TEACHING
RACQUETBALL

Steps to Success

Stan Kittleson, PhD
Augustana College
Rock Island, Illinois

Human Kinetics Publishers

אורה

Library of Congress Cataloging-in-Publication Data

Kittleson, Stan, 1934-
    Teaching racquetball : steps to success / Stan Kittleson.
       p. cm.
    ISBN 0-87322-533-3
    1. Racquetball--Coaching.   I. Title.
    GV1003.34.K56   1993
    796.34'3'07--dc20   93-15754
                                                  CIP

ISBN: 0-87322-533-3

Series Editor: Judy Patterson Wright
Developmental Editor: Rodd Whelpley
Assistant Editors: Valerie Hall, Moyra Knight, Dawn Roselund, and John Wentworth
Copyeditor: Merv Hendricks
Proofreader: Julia Anderson
Production Director: Ernie Noa
Typesetter: Kathy Boudreau-Fuoss
Text Design: Keith Blomberg
Text Layout: Denise Lowry and Tara Welsch
Cover Design: Jack Davis
Cover Photo: Will Zehr
Illustrations: Tom Janowski and Tim Offenstein
Printer: United Graphics

Instructional Designer for the Steps to Success Activity Series: Joan N. Vickers, EdD, University of Calgary, Calgary, Alberta, Canada

Human Kinetics books are available at special discounts for bulk purchase. Special editions or book excerpts can also be created to specification. For details, contact the Special Sales Manager at Human Kinetics.

Printed in the United States of America   10 9 8 7 6 5 4 3 2 1

Human Kinetics Publishers
Box 5076, Champaign, IL 61825-5076
1-800-747-4457

Canada: Human Kinetics Publishers, Box 24040, Windsor, ON N8Y 4Y9
1-800-465-7301 (in Canada only)

Europe: Human Kinetics Publishers (Europe) Ltd., P.O. Box IW14, Leeds LS16 6TR, England
0532-781708

Australia: Human Kinetics Publishers, P.O. Box 80, Kingswood 5062, South Australia
618-374-0433

New Zealand: Human Kinetics Publishers, P.O. Box 105-231, Auckland 1
(09) 309-2259

Contents

Series Preface

The Steps to Success Activity Series is a breakthrough in skill instruction through the development of complete learning progressions—the *steps to success*. These *steps* help individuals quickly perform basic skills successfully and prepare them to acquire more advanced skills readily. At each step, individuals are encouraged to learn at their own pace and to integrate their new skills into the total action of the activity.

The unique features of the Steps to Success Activity Series are the result of comprehensive development—through analyzing existing activity books, incorporating the latest research from the sport sciences, and consulting with students, instructors, teacher educators, and administrators. This groundwork pointed up the need for three different types of books—for participants, instructors, and teacher educators—which we have created and together comprise the Steps to Success Activity Series.

The participant's book, *Racquetball: Steps to Success*, is a self-paced, step-by-step guide that you can use as an instructional tool. The unique features of the participant's book include

- sequential illustrations that clearly show proper technique,
- helpful suggestions for detecting and correcting errors,
- excellent practice progressions with accompanying *Success Goals* for measuring performance, and
- checklists for rating technique.

A comprehensive instructor's guide, *Teaching Racquetball: Steps to Success*, accompanies the participant's book. This instructor's guide emphasizes how to individualize instruction. Each step of this instructor's guide promotes successful teaching and learning with

- teaching cues (Student Keys to Success) that emphasize fluidity, rhythm, and wholeness,
- criterion-referenced rating charts for evaluating a participant's initial skill level,
- suggestions for observing and correcting typical errors,
- tips for group management and safety,

- ideas for modifying the difficulty level,
- quantitative evaluations for all drills (*Success Goals*), and
- a test bank of written questions.

The series textbook, *Instructional Design for Teaching Physical Activities* (Vickers, 1990), explains the *steps to success* model, which is the basis for the Steps to Success Activity Series. Teacher educators can use the series textbook in their professional preparation classes to help future teachers and coaches learn how to design effective physical activity programs in school, recreation, or community teaching and coaching settings.

After identifying the need for various texts, we refined the *steps to success* instructional design model and developed prototypes. Once these prototypes were fine-tuned, we carefully selected authors for the activities who were not only thoroughly familiar with their sports but also had years of experience in teaching them. Each author had to be known as a gifted instructor who understands the teaching of sport so thoroughly that he or she could readily apply the *steps to success* model.

Next, all of the manuscripts were carefully developed to meet the guidelines of the *steps to success* model. Then our production team, along with outstanding artists, created a highly visual, user-friendly series of books.

The result: The Steps to Success Activity Series is the premier sports instructional series available today.

This series would not have been possible without the contributions of the following:

- Dr. Rainer Martens, Publisher
- Dr. Joan Vickers, instructional design expert,
- the staff of Human Kinetics Publishers, and
- the *many* students, teachers, coaches, consultants, teacher educators, specialists, and administrators who shared their ideas—and dreams.

Judy Patterson Wright
Series Editor

Preface

Your goal as a racquetball teacher and coach is to pass on enthusiasm for and knowledge of the game. You want to teach your students basic skills and use low-pressure drills and games to show them how to make good decisions in match situations. *Teaching Racquetball: Steps to Success* lets you give your students the best possible learning experience while you introduce them to a fast-paced, fun sport.

This book is primarily for people who teach college-level racquetball activity classes. I recall from my graduate student days two kinds of deficiencies among racquetball class instructors. Some instructors, although good physical educators, had little racquetball experience. Others, who were excellent racquetball players, had little teaching experience. Because this book is as much about teaching as it is about racquetball, it will help you whether your experience is in racquetball alone, teaching alone, or somewhere in between. It also is suitable for other settings. I hope that racquetball club professionals and high school teachers can adapt this book to their special needs. Regardless of the instructor's background or the setting, this book will be much more effective if students use the participant's book, *Racquetball: Steps to Success*.

After many years of teaching, I have concluded there are few original ideas. We learn from other teachers, from our students, from reading, from clinics, and from professional conferences. We modify basic ideas to suit our circumstances. I wish to thank all who shared their ideas and helped me learn racquetball and how to teach it, many of whom are unknown or unremembered. Thanks for giving me ideas and knowledge with which to pursue my love of teaching. Special thanks go to all the Augustana College students who taught me how to teach—and how people best learn. Most of all I have learned from my students that the best lessons contain elements of fun and accomplishment. When I mix in these elements, students amaze me with the pace of their progress.

Thanks also to Anne Williams, Leigh Ann Brown, Tammy Garwood, and Amanda Hall for their typing and computer work. I am grateful for their putting up with my spurts and stops of activity.

This book is dedicated to my wife, Judi, and my children, Steve, Paul, Jeanie, and Ryan.

Stan Kittleson

Implementing the Steps to Success Staircase

This book is meant to be flexible for both your students' needs and for yours. Some of the material can be covered in a different order, modified, or eliminated. We often hear that students' perceptions of a task change as the task is learned. But we often forget that teachers' perceptions and actions also change (Goc-Karp & Zakrajsek, 1987; Housner & Griffey, 1985; Imwold & Hoffman, 1983; Vickers, 1990).

Experienced teachers tend to use a common approach. First, they are highly organized (e.g., they don't waste time gathering groups or giving long explanations). Next, master teachers integrate information, from such fields as biomechanics, kinesiology, exercise physiology, motor learning, sport psychology, cognitive psychology, and instructional design. Next, they relate basic skills to the game or performance context, succinctly explaining their importance. Then, usually within a few minutes, they allow their students to practice steps that follow logical manipulations of factors such as

- the number of skills used in combination,
- the number of people used in tactical combinations (1 vs. 0, 1 vs. 1, 1 vs. 2, 2 vs. 0, 2 vs. 1, and 2 vs. 2),
- the addition or removal of equipment,
- court availability and other spatial restrictions,
- the use of targets,
- the size and distance of targets,
- the pace of the ball, and
- the rules.

This book shows you how basic racquetball skills interrelate with physiology, psychology, and other knowledge areas. (See Appendix A for an overview.) You can use this information to better understand interrelationships and to define the subject matter of each racquetball lesson. The following questions suggest ways to implement this knowledge base and help you improve teaching methods such as class organization, drills, objectives, progressions, and evaluations.

1. Under what conditions do you teach?
   - How much space is available?
   - What type of equipment is available?
   - What is the average class size?
   - How long is each class session?
   - How many class sessions do you teach?
   - Do you have teaching assistants?

2. What are your students' initial skill levels?
   - Look for rating charts located in the beginning of most steps (chapters) to identify criteria that discriminate between beginning, intermediate, and advanced levels.

3. What is the best order in which to teach (activity) skills?
   - Follow the sequence of steps (chapters) used in this book.
   - See Appendix B.1 for suggestions on when to introduce, review, or continue practicing each step (assuming a 50-minute class session).
   - Based on your answers to questions 1-3 above, use the form in Appendix B.2 to order the steps that you will be able to cover within your class time.

4. What objectives do you want your students to accomplish by the end of a lesson, unit, or course?
   - For technique or qualitative objectives, select from the Student Keys to Success that are provided for all basic skills [or see the Keys to Success Checklists in *Racquetball: Steps to Success*].
   - For performance or quantitative objectives, select from the Student Success Goals provided for each drill.
   - For written questions on racquetball strategy, rules, and techniques, select from the Test Bank.
   - See the Sample Individual Program (Appendix C.1) for selected technique and performance objectives for a 16-week unit.
   - For unit objectives, adjust the number of selected objectives to fit your unit length. (Use the form in Appendix C.2.)
   - For organizing daily objectives, see the sample Lesson Plan in Appendix D.1 and modify the basic lesson plan form in Appendix D.2 to fit your needs.

5. How will you evaluate your students?
   - Read the section "Evaluation Ideas."
   - Decide on a grading system: letter grades, pass-fail, total points, percentages, skill levels (bronze, silver, gold), and so forth.
6. Which activities should be selected to achieve student objectives?
   - Follow drills for each step because they are designed for four students per court and are presented in an easy-to-difficult order. Avoid selecting drills and exercises randomly.
   - Modify drills to best fit each student's skill level by following the suggestions for decreasing and increasing difficulty.
   - Ask your students to meet each drill's Success Goal.
   - For class assignments or makeups, use the cross-reference to the corresponding step and drill in the participant's book, *Racquetball: Steps to Success.*
7. What are your rules and expectations for the class?
   - For general management and safety guidelines, read the section "Preparing Your Class for Success."
   - For specific guidelines, read the subsection "Group Management and Safety Tips" included with each drill.
   - Tell your students your rules during orientation or the first day of class. Post the rules and discuss them often.

Teaching is a complex task that requires many decisions that affect both you and your students (Figure 1). Use this book to create an effective and successful learning experience for you and everyone you teach. And have fun too!

KEY

S = server
R = receiver
A = assistant
T = teacher
RHR = right-handed receiver
LHR = left-handed receiver
P = player
O = opponent
◉ = target for ball to hit
→ = path of player
- -▶ = path of ball
⊗ = retrievers, or students waiting for their turn to hit
P_1 = player 1, or the first person to hit the ball in a drill
P_2 = player 2, or the second person to hit the ball in a drill

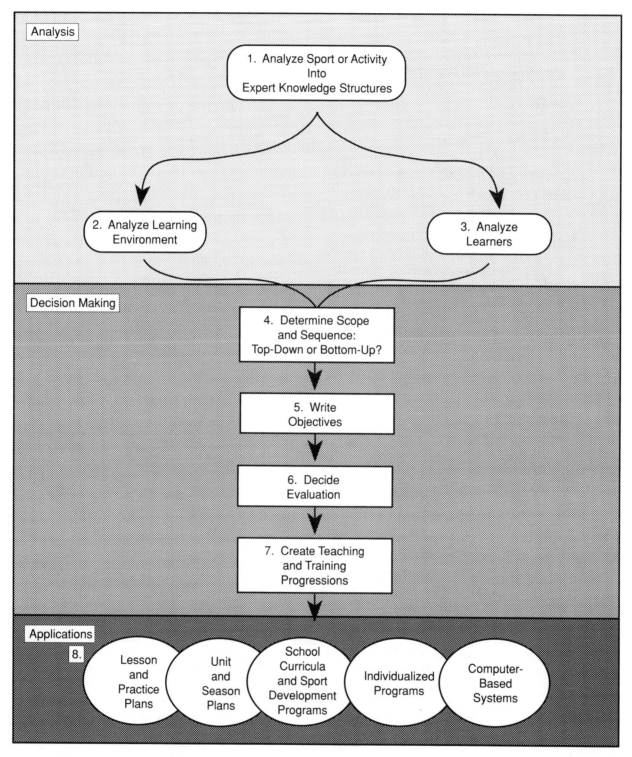

Figure 1   Instructional design model utilizing expert knowledge structures. *Note.* From *Instructional Design for Teaching Physical Activities* by J.N. Vickers, 1990, Champaign, IL: Human Kinetics. Copyright by Joan N. Vickers. Reprinted by permission. This instructional design model has appeared in earlier forms in *Badminton: A Structures of Knowledge Approach* (p. 1) by J.N. Vickers and D. Brecht, 1987, Calgary, AB: University Printing Services. Copyright 1987 by Joan N. Vickers; and "The Role of Expert Knowledge Structures in an Instructional Design Model for Physical Education" by J.N. Vickers, 1983, *Journal of Teaching in Physical Education*, **2**(3), p. 20. Copyright 1983 by Joan N. Vickers.

Preparing Your Class for Success

Successful teachers plan at two levels: They plan goals for the entire course, and they plan each lesson (and indeed each component of each lesson) so that it contributes to the overall course goals. *Teaching Racquetball: Steps to Success* is a source designed specifically to help you plan your course at both of these levels. Though the book is flexible enough for you to make adaptations to your needs, certain assumptions have been made in designing the text:

• You will be teaching students of varying ability. The book helps you identify players of beginning, intermediate, and advanced skill levels. All the drills presented include modifications for increased and decreased difficulty so that you can accommodate all students.

• You will have four students per court. Although it would be ideal to have only two players per court, four players, the maximum that should be assigned to a court, is the most prevalent (and most difficult) teaching situation, so many of the drills are designed for four players. Most, however, rotate students in and out of courts at short, regular intervals to minimize the tedium of waiting and to maximize the fun of playing.

PRECOURSE MANAGEMENT DECISIONS

If you are new to teaching racquetball, you may be surprised to find that some of your course management decisions have already been made by school or departmental policy, tradition, or the guidelines of other teachers. If you are lucky enough to work in a well-run program, then almost all pertinent decisions have been made for you, and you simply need to check with your supervisor to learn the policies. If not, you should consider the seven questions listed in "Implementing the Steps to Success Staircase." In any event, it is imperative that you spend time before the beginning of the term thinking about such things as your teaching conditions, your students' skill levels, the order in which you should teach racquetball skills, your course objectives, your evaluation methods, activity selection, and class rules.

It is equally important to consider the nuts and bolts of course management. Well before the term begins you should cover these bases:

• Check that enough courts have been reserved for your class. Make sure there are no schedule conflicts with other teachers, other departments, private groups, and so on. Also check to see whether the courts are in good playing condition and what steps you can take if they are not.

• Be sure you understand exactly how equipment for your course will be furnished. Some programs provide all the equipment for students; others require students to bring racquets and balls. Storage may be provided by the school or be the responsibility of the students.

• Check locker room facilities. Find out what provisions there are for storing and cleaning clothes and towels. As with the equipment, storage may be the responsibility of the school or the students.

• Establish a written dress code to give to students at the first meeting. Protective eye goggles should be at the top of the list of requirements.

• Prepare a written policy on absences and distribute it at the first meeting as well. (Some programs allow a predetermined number of absences without penalty, some have no policy, and others leave it to individual instructors to determine their own rules.) Whatever your situation, emphasize the policy and make class attendance necessary to pass the course: To learn and develop physical skills, a certain amount of time and practice is necessary. Be sure to apply your policy fairly by developing a routine for checking class attendance. Students may sit in bleachers near the courts, stand next to a fence or wall, or be assigned to courts.

• Make sure you know your program's policy on injuries; if it has none, establish your own in case a student becomes injured and cannot participate. You might give an "incomplete" grade, require the student to drop the course, allow written work to replace activity, or set a maximum grade that can be attained without full participation.

CREATING A MASTER LESSON PLAN FOR YOUR RACQUETBALL COURSE

Appendices B.1 and B.2 explain the use of the Scope and Teaching Sequence form, provide a sample sequence form that outlines a 28-meeting racquetball course, and provide a blank form for charting the master plan for your course. The sample master plan in Appendix B.1 has been developed primarily as a model for conducting a college-level course. Feel free to modify the outline to your class's specific needs. For example, if you are working strictly with beginners, you may need to spend some extra time on agility, throwing skills, remedial footwork, and weight transfer while hitting.

Always examine your plan with your students' needs in mind and make modifications as needed. But whatever your situation, it would be a good idea to incorporate the following advice into your master lesson plan:

• The first meeting should be organizational. Use it to give students a general idea of the game and a few basic rules.

• Spend only a small amount of time on the basic rules, in either the first or second class. Students with questions throughout the course can consult their books, ask you, or ask more experienced classmates while waiting for a turn on the court.

• In an early meeting, take 5 minutes to review basic rules and cover legal serves. After students have completed some of the service drills in Step 4, have them play 5-point matches to learn the game. (There are usually four students per court, so competitors change after every game.) Playing a number of these short games early in the term lets students put into practice—in spontaneous game situations that are hard to simulate with drills alone—all the skills you've covered so far as well as work on some new ones. It's also fun!

• Devote later meetings to tournament play. A "funnel tournament" is best for matching players of similar ability while allowing improving players to "challenge up." Use the funnel tournament format described in "Evaluation Ideas."

ON-COURT MANAGEMENT

I've provided some suggestions for organizing classes to make them interesting, productive, appropriately paced, and enjoyable. Above all, remember that you are teaching an *activity* course, not a lecture course.

Make sure there is always more practice than talking. Students can be actively learning even if they are not in the court: They can do simple ball-control drills, observe other players, read their books, chart other players, and offer suggestions to courtmates. All of these activities can be done during any waiting time.

Getting Classes Started

Begin your classes on time and keep things moving by following these procedures:

• Make players responsible for helping move equipment to and from the court before and after classes.

• Assign students to return racquets and balls if you have an equipment check-out area. If students must provide their own equipment, there will be little to do in this regard. All drills in this book (unless otherwise noted) assume that each player will have a racquet and that there will be a minimum of two balls per court available at all times; therefore, racquets and balls will generally not be listed in the equipment section of each drill.

• It is probably best to have your students warm up individually before class begins. Reinforce this policy often.

Warm-ups

Pages 9-13 of the participant's book, *Racquetball: Steps to Success*, describe warm-up activities. Encourage your students to use these exercises and to be ready for drills, activities, and play when class begins. Expecting your students to be warmed up when class starts can save a lot of time. A group warm-up during the first two class meetings will usually be enough to teach your students the procedure. Remind them to bring their books for reference and to do their warm-ups on their own after that.

Assigning home courts will help facilitate warm-ups. Each student will report to home court and complete three kinds of warm-up. As students' skill levels increase, their warm-ups also will progress. These commonly used warm up hitting routines are found in this book:

• Wall Rally (Step 3, Drill 3)
• Back Wall Toss (Step 11, Drill 1)
• Ceiling Shot Rally (Step 10, Drill 4)
• Down-the-Line Passes (Step 9, Drill 1)

- Chase the Rabbit (Step 11, Drill 4)
- Kill From Midcourt (Step 12, Drill 2)

Conducting Class

In each class, you will have a set of skills to cover. In accomplishing this teaching goal, keep in mind these points:

- Don't let students enter a court without protective eyewear.

- The nature of the racquetball courts dictates the teaching/learning style. You can have some group demonstrations and drills, but generally you'll call students to a central court for explanation and demonstration and then send them to their original, "home" courts for drill and practice. Interrupt games and call the class together three or four times per period; cover one skill or concept at a time. Cover smaller topics by visiting each court and by talking to students waiting their turns to play. Keep explanations and demonstrations brief.

- If you can't demonstrate some skills, there are other ways to handle the situation. Ask a student from a previous year's class to come in or select skilled students in your present class. Or use films, pictures, and videos.

- During the first or second meeting, group players in courts by their ability and/or experience. Call it their home court or some other name. It saves a lot of time if players know where to warm up or where to gather after group meetings. They will get to know each other faster, will progress faster, and will enjoy it more. Use students' results on the wall rally test (explained in the "Evaluation Ideas" section) to occasionally change their home courts. You can also change the courts as you observe them during drills. See the move-up tournament drill in Step 14 for another way to do this.

- Use low-key, fun games and activities as opposed to straight hitting drills. Many drills in this book can be converted easily into short, fun games, and you should encourage your students to make games out of the drills every chance you get. Inexperienced players need to have some success other than playing full-length games. Playing short games as drills reinforces concepts and adds fun to their learning. Only experienced or highly motivated players can concentrate easily on learning strokes without the incentives of games and activities.

- Be redundant. Cover the skills and concepts many times in different ways. This will be a new and unique sport for many of your students. Many will never have seen racquetball.

- Suggest corrections as soon as you see errors. If you don't, by the time the player is out of the court, other shots will have been hit and the critical teaching moment will have been lost. Be sure to wait until the rally is over before entering the court.

- In accuracy drills, use targets large enough to ensure that players will hit them (boxes or baskets, for example).

- Organize ball feeders and observers for drills to increase the number of serves or hits in the drills or games.

- Most weaker players and groups respond better to positive reinforcement than to critical remarks. As players become more sophisticated and secure in their games, they need less emotional stroking and more direct, helpful advice.

Finishing Classes

Finish classes with vigorous, demanding drills or competition and then gather the class for a meeting.

- How you call students together to dismiss them depends on how many courts you have and how they are arranged. You may want to notify each court yourself or send a student. Whistles, bells, or some other audible signals may also be used. Remember, this meeting is the time for closure and that last "teachable moment."

- The dismissal meeting is an excellent time to give positive comments to the group as a whole, set new objectives for the future, and give assignments to be completed before the next meeting.

- Name a player of the day and reward that player with recognition—an inexpensive prize or a special privilege.

- With children's groups, give racquet stickers or other rewards for good attendance, outstanding shots, reaching goals, best strategy, and so on.

- Encourage your students to observe other players outside class. Emphasize that they can learn a lot by watching others play.

- Use time effectively by having your students do some cool-down exercises while you talk to them during the dismissal meeting.

Cool-Down

Remind your students often to cool down after vigorous activity. The nature of your dismissal meeting will dictate how to handle this. Allow students who have just finished a strenuous drill or match to walk around during your post-class meeting and to stretch as you talk. If the meeting will be less than 3 minutes long, remind them to continue to cool down individually after the meeting. (For cool-down exercises, see *Racquetball: Steps to Success*, p. 13, "Cool-Down."

NINE LEGAL DUTIES

No teacher likes to think about the potential for an on-court mishap resulting in injury to a student and a lawsuit for the instructor. Nevertheless, it is prudent for teachers to protect themselves and their students by considering the guidelines that follow. Keep things in perspective, however, by recognizing your legal duties not just as ways to ward off legal liability but as tools to make your class a rewarding and safe learning experience.

1. Provide Adequate Supervision

This means that you must be at the courts during classes and practice sessions and that you must position yourself to see all players for as much of the class as possible. The logistics of racquetball courts may present unique challenges and opportunities. For instance, some courts are so enclosed they allow observation only from a window in the door. Other configurations may allow you to monitor many courts at once through a see-through wall or ceilingless design. These open configurations also allow you to shout down into the courts without physically disturbing the flow of the game or drill. Regardless of your teaching environment, your students have a right to expect that they will be conscientiously monitored and that you will be nearby to handle problems.

2. Plan Soundly

The gradual, cumulative progression presented in this text and the participant's book is essential: Plan skill instruction, practices, and drills so your players do not move too rapidly into techniques or contests beyond their skill levels. Improvement that is consistent with readiness should be the goal. Plan a sequence of activities that students can reasonably be expected to perform.

Consider physical skills, physical condition, court availability, and time allotment when planning lessons. The variety of drills for beginners will be limited until they can exchange hits rapidly using a variety of shots. As players develop, expect them to accomplish more in less time. This lets you use a wider range of class activities. Rushing your students to learn skills for which they aren't ready is bad pedagogy and invites more chances for injury. Push your students toward excellence, but use sound, safe educational planning to reach your teaching goals.

3. Anticipate Inherent Risks

With as many as four people, four racquets, and one fast-moving rubber ball enclosed in a 40-foot by 20-foot room, racquetball carries the obvious risk of players being hit by a ball or racquet. Other racquetball risks are presented by vigorous exercise affecting the respiratory, muscular, skeletal, and cardiovascular systems. You must warn your players of these risks and minimize dangers by providing a safe environment.

You might try to minimize your legal liability by having students sign a consent form acknowledging racquetball's inherent risks, but realize that an informed consent statement will not protect you or your institution in a trial if negligence can be proved.

4. Keep Courts Safe

Providing a safe environment requires not just safe racquetball courts but also properly used equipment.

It is your responsibility to inspect your facility regularly and thoroughly. Do not allow students to play on dusty or slick courts and avoid overcrowding courts. If you are teaching at the college level, work with the administration to limit the number of students per court. Four players per court is reasonable; anything higher can present morale problems and will challenge your ability to keep students active and safe.

Common injuries associated with racquetball include being struck in the eye with a ball, falling on the court, and being hit with a racquet (either the player's own racquet or someone else's). Some of these injuries will be avoided if you enforce safety rules. First, allow no player on the court without goggles. Second, be sure every player has secured the racquet's safety thong on his or her wrist. Third, make sure students understand that it is both within their rights and their duty to call hinders (which are explained in the participant's book). Stress to them that it is always better to replay a point than to risk injury. Finally, do not tolerate players who, either out of frustration or elation, hit the ball after the point is decided. The opponent's guard naturally is down after the point is over, and so the potential for injury is high.

5. Evaluate Students' Abilities and Disabilities

Look out for students' injuries or incapacities and determine whether limiting participation is appropriate. Your institution may have already established such policies in this area, and it is your duty to be aware of them. If there is no policy, develop your own for your classes. A common-sense approach would be to announce to the class that anyone who has a physical or emotional problem should privately advise you. Then you can plan lessons accordingly and lessen the likelihood of injury or illness.

Allow players with disabilities to participate in the least restrictive environment possible, and, as with all athletes, encourage them to compete at the highest level their developing skills allow. Players with respiratory problems should be warned that strenuous racquetball activities may complicate these conditions. In areas of high temperatures and humidity, students should be warned about dehydration and exhaustion. Water should be readily available for all students.

6. Match Opponents by Ability

In all physical activities, grouping players by ability makes drills, activities, and competition more productive. As a legal issue, keeping students evenly matched by size and ability is relevant only in contact sports. Accidents most likely to occur in racquetball because of unequal ability among players include the lesser experienced player getting hit by a hard-hit ball or colliding with an opponent. See the move-up

drill in Step 14 to lessen the probability of this type of accident.

7. Prepare First Aid Procedures

Provide first aid equipment and establish emergency medical procedures that can be put into action immediately. Keep a well-stocked first aid kit where you can get to it quickly; it is best if the kit is at courtside. Items most likely to be needed are Band-aids, bandages, elastic wraps, and ice (or chemical cold-packs). Post emergency phone numbers near the courts so you can call for specialized help right away.

8. Protect Student Civil Rights

Students' civil rights are guaranteed on and off the racquetball court. Our judicial system requires you to assure that your students' basic rights are not violated. It is no longer easy to place restrictions on students' appearances or expressions, but appropriate dress and behavior can still be expected and enforced, especially to prevent injuries. In the event of a dispute, follow due process principles. Every school should ensure that teachers and students can have their sides heard.

9. Be Prepared Legally

No matter how careful you are, be aware that students do get injured, and that injuries may result in litigation. Such lawsuits can result in damage amounts far beyond the means of most teachers or coaches. It is a good idea to carry adequate personal liability insurance.

In the event of an injury, you can minimize your legal risk by providing prudent first aid, reporting every injury to the proper authorities as soon after the incident as possible, filling out proper paperwork (and making copies for yourself), and seeing that reports reach the correct school administrators. In such situations, make notes while the events are fresh. Don't trust memory for details of events that occurred months or years before a deposition, hearing, or trial.

Step 1   The Grips—Forehand, Backhand, Continental

This step teaches your students the techniques of a good grip. Impress upon them how vital a good grip is to success at racquetball, specifically that it is essential to developing skill and controlling the ball.

The Eastern forehand and backhand should be recommended to all students, but if they have trouble changing grips, the Continental grip will let them start learning the game. Ask them to select a grip to try for a week or two. If problems persist, you may recommend they try another grip.

Your students will exhibit a wide range of experience: Some will have played a lot of racquetball, and others will never have held a racquet. Even experienced players need occasionally to review their grip, so a little time spent on the grip now can yield dividends later.

You might ask experienced players to help beginners. Keep the lesson short and try to make it fun. For example, with the "frying pan" grip, you can make reference to cooking or scooping ice cream. You can get an early idea of your students' ability by how quickly they master these simple tasks and by how they swing the racquet.

Step 1 should be taught in the same lesson as Step 2 because they are closely related. Coverage of Step 1 should take from 5 to 10 minutes depending upon your students' experience. Don't spend too much time on Step 1, because in Step 2 and Step 3 you can observe players who are having trouble and refer them back to Step 1 for remedial work. One of the worst teaching errors is trying to teach someone something they already know.

STUDENT KEYS TO SUCCESS

- Hold racquet in fingers.
- "Shake hands" with racquet.
- Position fingers diagonally across handle.
- Position V consistently.

Grip Rating

CHECKPOINT	BEGINNING LEVEL	INTERMEDIATE LEVEL	ADVANCED LEVEL
Grip	• Does not remember grip described • Has trouble returning V to proper position when changing grips	• Understands grip • Usually can return V to proper position when changing grips	• Consistent grip • Consistent V position when changing grips
Finger Control	• Fingers perpendicular to handle • Wrist too stiff during swing • Cannot extend wrist to point racquet at a target	• Fingers diagonally across handle • Wrist sometimes stiff on backhand grip and serving • Angle too great when pointing racquet	• Racquet held in fingers • Good wrist action • Good wrist extension
Tension	• Usually fingers are too tight	• Sometimes forgets to relax grip	• Can relax grip and retain control

Error Detection and Correction for the Grip

Remember that instead of spending a great deal of time on this step you merely want to establish a good foundation that you can refer to later. It is better to get your students into active drills and then to correct improper grips individually for the few who have trouble.

ERROR

CORRECTION

1. Grip is so tight at all times that fingernails show white.

2. Student has loose grip. Racquet slips out of hand while swinging.

3. Forehand stroke seems OK. On backhand stroke, racquet is not vertical through the hitting zone.

4. Wrist is stiff or restricted when swinging racquet.

5. Student holds racquet handle too deep in the palm of hand. Racquet forms right angle with forearm.

1. Have student tighten grip to maximum, then relax tension. Repeat several times. Then tell student to relax pressure between swings. Fingers will tighten naturally when swinging.

2. Tell student to hold tightly and hit the racquet on the strings with the heel of the off hand to check grip firmness. The racquet should not shake in the hand.

3. The student may be using the frying pan grip or forgetting to change to a backhand grip. Have experienced players help others. Use a marker to outline the V of the hand. Use chalk to mark the correct bevel of the handle.

4. Check to see that students are holding the racquet in their fingers. [See *Racquetball*, Step 1, Drill 5.] You may have to move the racquet to a position in the fingers.

5. Ask student to point head of racquet at target. He or she will not be able to point directly with the head. Then you can physically move the grip into the fingers. [See *Racquetball*, Step 1, Drills 5 and 6.]

Grip Drills

Before you lead your students in the drills, space them so they have room to swing without hitting someone. Don't expect them to try grips without swinging racquets. In fact, swinging the racquet is necessary for completing some drills.

1. *Frying Pan*
[Corresponds to *Racquetball*, Step 1, Drill 1]

Group Management and Safety Tips

- Have students form a semicircle in front of you.
- Allow 1 to 2 minutes for this drill.

Instructions to Class

- "Lay your racquet flat on the floor. Now pick up your racquet. See how the V between your thumb and forefinger is on the large flat part of the handle that was facing up? This is the last time I want to see the V in that position. Now take five swings with your forehand and five with your backhand.

Remember how this incorrect grip feels, especially for the backhand swing."

Student Option

- "Repeat as often as desired."

Student Success Goal

- 10 swings with incorrect grip

To Decrease Difficulty

- Not applicable

To Increase Difficulty

- Not applicable

2. Grip Checks
[Corresponds to *Racquetball*, Step 1, Drills 2, 3, 4]

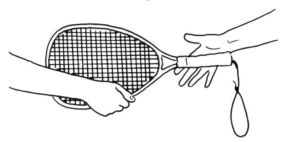

Group Management and Safety Tips

- Have students form a semicircle in front of you.
- Select partner.
- Allow 3 to 4 minutes for drills.

Instructions to Class

- "Stand facing your partner. Hold the racquet face perpendicular to the floor. Extend the handle to your partner. Partner, extend your arm as if to 'shake hands.' Grasp the handle so the V between thumb and forefinger is on the top back bevel of the handle. The first partner should check the grip and then exchange places. After each of you has had the grip checked, practice switching from forehand grip to backhand grip. Check each other's grip repeatedly."

Student Options

- "You can practice the 'shake hands' grip alone. Hold the racquet with the nongrip hand. Place your grip hand open against the strings of the face of the racquet. Slide the grip hand down the handle and assume the grip."

- "Turn your hand so your palm is up. Open your hand partly so your partner can see your lifeline in the palm of your hand while you still have control of the racquet in your finger. Then repeat with the backhand grip." [See *Racquetball*, Step 1, Drill 5.]
- "Assume a forehand grip with finger control. Straighten your arm and point your racquet toward a target. If you have a proper grip and finger control, the racquet handle should look like an extension of your arm. Partners should check this from the side." [See *Racquetball*, Step 1, Drill 6.]

Student Success Goals

- Practices and learns forehand and backhand grips and learns to feel them without visually checking grips
- 10 correct grips forehand, backhand, and changing grips

To Decrease Difficulty

- Not applicable

To Increase Difficulty

- Not applicable

3. *Identification of Grip Drill*
[New Drill]

Group Management and Safety Tips

- Have students in a semicircle in front of you.
- Allow 1 to 2 minutes for this drill.

Equipment

- 1 racquet for demonstrator

Instructions to Class

- "I will assume an Eastern forehand, an Eastern backhand, a Continental grip, or a frying pan grip. When you recognize the grip, raise your hand and I will call on you to identify it. The first one to correctly identify the grip gets to demonstrate the next grip."

Student Options

- "You can do this drill in smaller groups."
- "You can do this while waiting for a court."

Student Success Goals

- Correctly identify each grip.
- Be the first to identify each grip.

To Decrease Difficulty

- Limit choices to Eastern forehand, Eastern backhand, and Continental.
- Teacher can demonstrate all the time.

To Increase Difficulty

- Put a time limit (such as 5 seconds) upon viewing the grip.
- Show grip only while swinging at an imaginary ball.

4. *Incorrect Grip Identification*
[New Drill]

Group Management and Safety Tips

- Have students in a semicircle in front of you.
- Allow 2 to 3 minutes for this drill.

Equipment

- 1 racquet for demonstrator

Instructions to Class

- "I will assume an incorrect grip and announce it as a correct grip. I might also have other errors that are in your text. You must recognize the error and tell me how to correct it. The first one to do this correctly gets to demonstrate the next error."

Student Options

- "You can do this drill in smaller groups."
- "Do this while waiting for a court."
- "Mimic the error with your own racquet to help you identify how the error feels."

Student Success Goals

- Correctly identify and correct the error.
- Be the first to correctly identify and correct the error.

To Decrease Difficulty

- Call on students who can answer correctly.
- Teacher can demonstrate all the time.

To Increase Difficulty

- Place a time limit (such as 3 to 4 seconds) on the opportunity to respond.
- Show the error only while swinging at an imaginary ball.

Step 2   Developing Control of the Ball

You will find your students have a wide range of ability in controlling the direction of the ball. Some will have excellent hand–eye coordination; others will need a lot of practice to develop it. In Step 2 you'll start your students thinking about just where they want to place the ball rather than simply returning it to the front wall. If you emphasize this concept often, your students will become better players sooner. Power (hitting the ball hard) is important at certain times and at certain levels of play, but control (hitting the ball where you want it to go) is important at every level, and it is always more important than power. As you cover subsequent steps, students will learn where to direct the ball depending on the situation and the location of the opponent.

A discussion of the racquet angle and the direction of the ball impresses on students the need for proper positioning to control the ball. Most will not have thought about this aspect, although some will automatically position themselves and angle the racquet face correctly. Start your discussion of ball control by explaining that at the moment of contact of racquet to ball, the body should be facing the side wall. This is true for both forehand and backhand shots.

Then talk about how the angle of the racquet face determines the direction of the ball. Remember to point out two factors: position of the body relative to the ball at contact, and wrist and forearm action. Remind players that (for right-handed players attempting forehand shots) to make the ball go left, they contact the ball in front of the front hip and close the racquet face.

To make the ball go right, they open the racquet face and contact the ball behind the front hip. To make the ball go straight, they contact the ball even with the front hip and keep the racquet face square. Be sure to show any left-handed players how they need to contact the ball to send it left, right, and straight ahead. Beginners usually understand these concepts in theory, but often are not aware whether their own racquet faces are open or closed at impact. [See *Racquetball*, Figures 2.1-2.5 for an explanation of closed, square, and open racquet faces.]

So, as you observe racquetball players, you will see that many attempt to return the ball without positioning themselves properly. Even highly skilled players need to progress from the initial stage of merely returning the ball to the front wall to the point where they are consciously directing it to the most advantageous location.

Getting students through this first stage is one of your most important jobs as a racquetball instructor. Many players remain at an intermediate level because they are unable or unwilling to use less power and more control. Proper emphasis at this step will help all your students progress more rapidly.

STUDENT KEYS TO SUCCESS

- Use proper grip.
- Concentrate on developing "touch" or control.
- Control racquet angle and body position to control ball.

Developing Control Rating

CHECKPOINT	BEGINNING LEVEL	INTERMEDIATE LEVEL	ADVANCED LEVEL
Distance From Ball	• Often too close or too far away	• Usually correct distance from ball	• Consistently correct distance from ball
Power	• Often hits too hard or too soft • Ball often contacted off center ("sweet spot") of racquet • Arm movement jerky and inconsistent	• Usually applies correct power • Usually hits sweet spot • Follow-through sometimes not smooth	• Good "touch" • Consistently hits sweet spot • Smooth swing and follow-through
Direction of Ball	• Loses control of ball often • Has little feel for position of body with respect to ball • Cannot move and keep ball under control	• Loses control of ball occasionally • Usually good body position • Must move quickly to maintain position and control of ball	• Opens and closes racquet face to control ball (Figures 2.1 and 2.2) • Excellent positioning • Strokes ball and easily moves into position to play the next shot

Figure 2.1   A closed face causes the ball to go left.

Figure 2.2   An open face sends the ball right.

Error Detection and Correction for Developing Ball Control

These errors are very elementary but could alert you to students who may have perceptual motor difficulties. Be patient with them, and encourage them to be patient with themselves. Reassure them that they can improve, but they may need a bit more practice than other players. You could also use information gained here to group students by ability so more-skilled players are not held back in their progress nor are less-skilled players intimidated by those who are better. The drills that follow will help you identify and correct these errors.

ERROR 🚫

CORRECTION

1. Student is often too close to or too far from ball; elbow of racquet arm is too close to or too far from body.

1. Hold or bounce ball proper distance away to contact ball with center of racquet face and with arm extended.

2. Arm movement is jerky and inconsistent; too much or too little power.

2. Physically guide student's arm movement.

3. Student cannot move and maintain control of ball.

3. Have student practice stationary activity until control improves.

Racquet Control Drills

1. Ball Dribble

[Corresponds to *Racquetball*, Step 2, Drills 1 and 2]

Group Management and Safety Tips

- Drill can be done on any level floor.
- Have students spread out to allow sufficient room.
- Allow 2 to 4 minutes of practice.
- Suggest variations for students who achieve the goal immediately.
- Suggest students do this drill while waiting for court time.

Equipment

- Racquets, 1 per student
- Balls, 1 per student

Instructions to Class

- "Hold the racquet with a forehand grip and practice dribbling the ball on the floor. Try to keep the ball about waist high, and stay within a small area. Now try to keep your left foot, or your right foot if you're a left-hander, in place while retaining control of the ball. Finally, try this drill walking or running around the court or on any designated path. Next, turn your palm up and practice dribbling in the air. Keep the ball under control by bumping it 6 to 12 inches off the racquet. Try the same variations as the floor dribble, keeping one foot in place and then walking or running. Lastly, try using alternate sides of the racquet face while standing in one place."

Student Options

- "Set your own goals for the number of repetitions."
- "Use a certain number of seconds or minutes (1 or 2) as the duration of the drill."

Student Success Goals

- 25 consecutive floor dribbles in each of three ways
- 25 consecutive air dribbles in each of four ways without losing control of ball

To Decrease Difficulty

- Have student choke up on racquet handle.
- Allow student to bounce ball between air dribbles.
- Reduce the Success Goals to 15 or 20 dribbles.

To Increase Difficulty

- Increase the Success Goals by increments of 5.
- Have student alternate ground and air dribbles.
- Have student use the edge of the racquet [*Racquetball*, Step 2, Drill 3].
- Have student alternate dribbles with a partner.

2. *Wall Rally*

[Corresponds to *Racquetball*, Step 2, Drill 4]

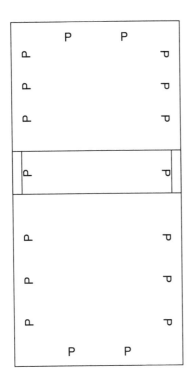

Group Management and Safety Tips

- Have students spread out to allow sufficient room.
- Any straight wall will do.
- You may have to send students to their "home courts."
- Allow 3 to 5 minutes of practice.
- Demonstrate the drill if possible.

Equipment

- Racquets, 1 per person
- Balls, 1 per person

Instructions to Class

- "Stand 4 or 5 feet from the wall. Tap the ball softly against the wall. Play it on one bounce and return it to the wall. Keep it in play. Start with your forehand grip and keep the ball to your forehand side. Then, repeat the drill using only your backhand. Next, try alternating your forehand and backhand strokes. Remember to change grips. Finally, you can play the ball on the fly or volley and keep it in the air. Remember to stroke the ball softly in order to keep control."

Student Options

- "Set your own goal for the number of repetitions."
- "Play a game with a partner, adding total strokes together."
- "Compete with others to see who can get highest total."

Student Success Goal

- 25 consecutive returns in each of the four ways (forehand, backhand, alternating forehand and backhand, and volley) without losing control

To Decrease Difficulty

- Choke up on racquet.
- Let ball bounce more than once if necessary.
- Have student move closer to wall.
- Reduce the Success Goal.

To Increase Difficulty

- Have student move farther from wall.
- Increase Success Goal.
- Have someone try to distract student's attention.

3. Angle Control

[Corresponds to *Racquetball*, Step 2, Drill 5]

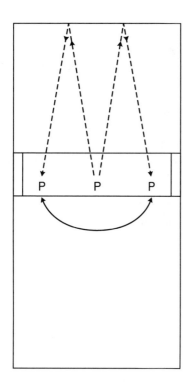

Group Management and Safety Tips

- Only two students can do this drill at one time in each court.
- Drill can be done anywhere there is a straight wall and sufficient room.
- Caution hitter to hit softly so partner can catch the ball.
- Demonstrate the drill if possible.
- Allow 5 to 6 minutes of practice.
- Other students can assist by collecting missed balls.
- Remove any tape or chalk marks immediately after class.

Equipment

- Balls, 5 per court
- Racquets, 1 per person
- Colored tape or chalk to mark targets on front wall (to decrease difficulty)

Instructions to Class

- "Stand in the service area near the center line. Drop the ball and stroke it to the front wall so it rebounds to your partner who is standing in the service area near the left wall. Face the right wall and use your fore-hand stroke. You will have to drop the ball forward of your body so the racquet face can close as it contacts the ball. Hit the ball softly with control so your partner can catch it after one bounce. Next, the catcher will move to the right wall. Still using your fore-hand grip, turn your body slightly and contact the ball nearer your rear hip so your racquet face is slightly open on contact. Remember to hit the ball softly with control."
- "Repeat these two drills using your back-hand stroke and dropping the ball on the backhand side of your body. Before you hit each shot, try to visualize the path the ball must take to reach your partner. This will help you also visualize the spot on the front wall where your ball must hit."
- "When you have hit both forehands and backhands switch jobs with your partner so your partner can practice hitting, too."

Student Options

- "Allow catching partner to trap ball between racquet and other hand."
- "Cooperate to see how many in a row you can do successfully."
- "Form teams of two and compete against courtmates or others."

Student Success Goal

- Hit 10 shots within 4 or 5 feet of partner's position in each of four ways: to left, then to right using forehand; and to left, then to right using backhand.

To Decrease Difficulty

- Change Success Goal to any part of left or right side of court.
- Move starting positions closer to front wall.
- Change criteria to include catching ball after any number of bounces.
- Mark target areas on front wall with colored tape or chalk.

To Increase Difficulty

- Do not allow catcher to move to catch ball.
- Move hitter and catcher farther away from front wall.
- Do not allow ball to hit the side wall before reaching catcher.

Step 3 Basic Strokes—Forehand and Backhand

Because the forehand and backhand are the basis of all racquetball shots, all players need to master them. But lengthy explanations and theoretical discussions will only bore your students. Because many students won't understand the fundamentals involved, just stress that these strokes are the foundation and move on to the drills where students can see the need for proper fundamentals. At the proper time, encouragement from you can motivate students to return to this section and study the fundamentals in more detail. Remember that everyone learns at their own pace and in different ways.

FOREHAND

Most players rapidly develop a decent forehand. Less-skilled players take a little longer to learn. It is possible and permissible to "run around your backhand" in racquetball much more than in tennis. The court is smaller, and with a little extra effort players can get back into position quicker.

Spend enough time on the forehand and stress the Keys to Success. Beginning players should develop the forehand as one shot they can depend on and as a foundation on which to build their game.

BACKHAND

Almost everyone has a weaker backhand than forehand. Even so, there is no reason why it cannot be a solid shot. Just remind your students that the Keys to Success are the same for both shots. If a student improves the backhand so that it is stronger than someone else's, he or she will have an advantage. Don't discourage players who want to try a two-handed backhand as in tennis. But, as they drill and improve their backhand, they will gradually abandon the two-handed shot. The need for quickness, reach, and good wrist action are reasons you may use to explain why a one-handed backhand is stronger. As they play, they will probably figure it out for themselves.

Plenty of time spent in drills with the backhand will develop skill and confidence. With that will come victories and satisfaction for your students.

STUDENT KEYS TO SUCCESS

- Take ready position.
- Focus eyes on ball.
- Start backswing early.
- Keep weight on back foot.
- Face side wall.
- Step toward target.
- Transfer weight.
- Swing through ball.
- Return to ready position.

Forehand and Backhand Rating

CHECKPOINT	BEGINNING LEVEL	INTERMEDIATE LEVEL	ADVANCED LEVEL
Preparation	• Not in ready position—tries to run around most backhand shots	• Usually ready—runs around too many backhand shots	• Good ready position—runs around a few shots. Good footwork for backhand
	• Late moving into position for shot	• Usually in good position for shot on time	• Gets to ball early
	• Faces front wall	• Usually faces side wall	• Faces side wall at contact
	• Backswing is short and late	• Backswing usually starts on time	• Takes racquet back early and smoothly
	• Weight not on rear foot	• Weight transfer to rear foot sometimes limited and not always smooth	• Weight on rear foot and plants rear foot firmly
	• Forgets to change grips (if using Eastern grips)	• Usually changes grips	• Always has proper grip
Execution	• Eyes not on ball	• Eyes usually on ball	• Eyes pick up ball early and remain fixed while moving
	• Little shoulder or hip rotation	• Limited shoulder and hip rotation	• Shoulders and hip rotate fully during shot
	• Wrist stiff all through shot	• Some wrist action after contact	• Good release of wrist at contact
	• Racquet arm usually bent at elbow	• Some arm extension and elbow straighter	• Racquet arm fully extended
	• Erratic contact of racquet with ball	• Some off-center hits	• Shots consistently hit on sweet spot
	• Racquet face often open	• Better timing of hit and racquet face usually OK	• Racquet face consistently faces in proper direction and good control of ball
	• Weight transfer to rear foot while swinging	• Weight transfer to front foot sometimes early or late	• Smooth weight transfer from rear to front foot and good timing
	• Little power on shots	• Some power but not always consistent	• Can hit with power consistently
	• Head and eyes move a lot during swing	• Head and eyes stay focused on the ball most of the time and head moves occasionally	• Head and eyes stay focused on the ball during swing

Forehand and Backhand Rating

CHECKPOINT	BEGINNING LEVEL	INTERMEDIATE LEVEL	ADVANCED LEVEL
Follow-Through	• Racquet and arm usually stop at contact • Very little weight transfer or reverse transfer from front to rear foot • Stands and watches shot	• Smoother swing with racquet and arm continuing after contact • Weight transfer from rear to front foot and sometimes squares body to front wall • Hesitates before moving, but does regain balance and is ready to move	• Racquet arm fully extended and comes across body to start squaring up for return to ready position • Smooth weight transfer and squares body into ready position • Moves into good ready position without hesitation

Error Detection and Correction for the Forehand and Backhand

There are many possible errors on the forehand stroke. Help students with major problems, but let most try to correct the small ones themselves. It is more important that students get on-task practice and try to learn from the results of their shots.

For backhand errors, first check the players' hands. Most beginners forget to change to a backhand grip. Tell them to use the opposite hand to assist in changing the grip. Experienced players can often switch grips without using the opposite hand. Students using the Continental grip, of course, won't change grips for shots. The best attitude for teacher and student is to be patient and practice a lot. The backhand shot is difficult for most players and takes time to develop.

ERROR

CORRECTION

1. Student has trouble getting weight on rear foot.

1. Have student lift front foot off floor before starting stroke.

ERROR 🚫   **CORRECTION**

2. Student faces front wall all during shot, resulting in arm shot with poor control and power.

2. Review shoulder and hip rotation. Tell student to show back to front wall during preparation. Face side wall at contact.

3. Student has trouble keeping eyes on ball.

3. Put numbers on balls with marking pencil. Have student hit ball and then report number.

4. Not much wrist action or power.

4. Don't worry about it. Control is more important at this stage. Power will come with practice.

5. Not much forward weight transfer.

5. Have student step toward front wall with rear foot after every shot.

ERROR	**CORRECTION**

6. Student uses wrong grip. V of thumb and forefinger not at correct spot on handle.

6. Physically show correct grip (Eastern or Continental). Have student hit 10 shots in a row with correct grip. Make sure the thumb is not placed flat against the back part of the racquet handle on backhand. (See Step 1, Drill 2.)

7. General lack of control on shots.

7. Check grip. Remind student to contact ball near front hip. This requires better footwork and positioning. [Review *Racquetball*, Step 1, Drill 1.]

Forehand and Backhand Drills

1. *Forehand and Backhand Swings*
[New Drill]

Group Management and Safety Tips

- Find an area large enough for entire class. Racquetball court may be too small.
- Position students so they do not hit each other's racquets.
- To demonstrate, face away from students.
- Have an assistant or student demonstrate so you can observe students from behind if possible.
- Occasionally have students freeze on command so you can check racquet and body positions.

Instructions to Class

- "Line up in columns and rows facing the front wall. Follow the example and go through these steps as I swing with a forehand or backhand stroke: ready, pivot, step, swing, and recover. Try to exactly imitate the swing you see demonstrated in front of you."

Student Option

- "Either watch me and imitate the swing, or visualize yourself hitting as you move in response to the commands."

Student Success Goal

- 50 swings, alternating 25 forehand and 25 backhand, all with good form

To Decrease Difficulty

- Have students work as partners and help each other.
- Let students step aside and observe or go through motions at a slower pace.
- Demonstrator slows pace of steps.

To Increase Difficulty

- Increase the number of swings.
- Increase the pace of the commands.

2. "Big Swoosh"

[Corresponds to *Racquetball*, Step 3, Drill 1]

Group Management and Safety Tips

- Review safety rules about swinging racquets.
- Remind students to use safety thong.
- Space players a safe distance apart.
- Use a large space.
- May have to send students to their home courts for this drill.

Equipment

- 1 racquet per person (no balls needed)

Instructions to Class

- "Practice your forehand and backhand strokes without a ball. Try to develop a smooth stroke with proper wrist action. If you get good wrist action and racquet head speed, you should hear your racquet 'swoosh' at the moment you would be hitting the ball."

Student Option

- "Do this with a partner."

Student Success Goal

- 50 total strokes (25 strokes with forehand swing, 25 strokes with backhand)

To Decrease Difficulty

- Decrease Success Goal.

To Increase Difficulty

- Increase Success Goal.
- Count only strokes that "swoosh" loudly.

3. Wall Rally

[Corresponds to *Racquetball*, Step 3, Drill 2]

Group Management and Safety Tips

- Allow only one player per court for this drill. Others can be in court as observers.
- Observers can save time by retrieving balls for hitter.
- Any straight wall with a smooth floor can be used to minimize waiting time.
- This drill makes an excellent skill test. A modification of it appears in the "Evaluation Ideas" section.
- All players on the court rotate positions to ball chaser, feeder, and hitter.

Instructions to Class

- "Stay behind the short line. Drop the ball to the floor. As it rebounds, hit it to the front wall. When it rebounds from the front wall, move into position and return it to the front wall again. You may play the ball in the air or after any bounce. Continue for as many consecutive times as you can without losing control. Use either forehand or backhand stroke as necessary. Don't swing too hard, just swing smoothly and try to keep the ball in play. Stay behind the short line."

Student Options

- "Increase or decrease the distance from the front wall."
- "Use the forehand only."
- "Alternate the forehand and backhand."
- "Use the backhand only."

Student Success Goals

- 20 consecutive returns without losing control
- 15 consecutive forehand returns without losing control
- 10 consecutive backhand returns without losing control

To Decrease Difficulty

- Decrease distance from front wall.
- Reduce Success Goals by 5 or 10.

To Increase Difficulty

- Increase distance from front wall.
- Increase Success Goals by 5 or 10.
- Time the number of returns in 30 seconds.
- Use forehand stroke only.
- Use backhand stroke only.

4. Side-Wall Toss
[Corresponds to *Racquetball*, Step 3, Drill 3]

Group Management and Safety Tips

- Review safety rules.
- Have one student hit forehand shots from one side wall and another hit backhand shots from the other side wall at the same time.

Instructions to Class

- "Stand 4 to 5 feet from the side wall on your forehand side at midcourt. Toss the ball to the side wall 2 or 3 feet high. As the ball bounces, get into position and return it to the front wall with a forehand stroke. Catch the return and make another toss to the side wall for a second shot."
- "A second person can be using the other wall at the same time. Exchange positions so you can practice both forehand and backhand."
- "Try to control your shot so the ball remains on your half of the court."

- "Courtmates can retrieve the balls while waiting their turns."

Student Options

- "Have a contest with a person on the other side for speed or accuracy."
- "Keep a personal record of your most consecutive good returns to front wall."

Student Success Goal

- 50 returns to the front wall (25 forehands and 25 backhands)

To Decrease Difficulty

- Decrease Success Goal.
- Move closer to front wall.

To Increase Difficulty

- Increase Success Goal.
- Move farther from front wall.
- Count only shots that stay in your half of the court.

5. *Partner Forehand-Backhand*

[Corresponds to *Racquetball*, Step 3, Drill 4]

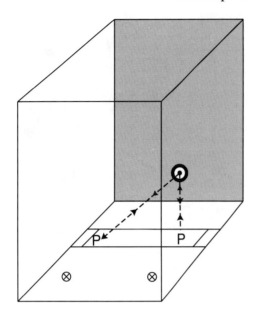

Group Management and Safety Tips

- Only two players play per court. Others can be in court as observers and ball chasers.
- Observers can have extra balls for hitters when control is lost.
- Remove tape from wall after drill.

Equipment

- Tape a target to center of front wall approximately 4 feet high. Use colored tape or chalk or paper.

Instructions to Class

- "Both players stand near the short line, one on each side of an imaginary midline. Forehand player hits ball softly off the targeted area on the front wall to partner's backhand. Backhand player returns the ball to partner's forehand side. Continue the rally until each has hit 10 shots. Then exchange positions for 10 more shots each."

Student Options

- "Increase or decrease the distance from the front wall."
- "Make a competitive contest out of the drill."
- "Do the drill by yourself, moving quickly from one position to the other."

Student Success Goal

- 20 consecutive shots without losing control (10 each player)

To Decrease Difficulty

- Decrease distance from front wall.
- Decrease angle: Both players stay near midline.
- Partner catches ball then drops and strokes the ball to return it.
- Decrease Success Goal.

To Increase Difficulty

- Increase distance from front wall.
- Increase angle: Both players move closer to side walls.
- Increase Success Goal.

6. Five-Point Partner Rally
[Corresponds to *Racquetball*, Step 3, Drill 5]

Group Management and Safety Tip

- Have only two players inside the court. Others should watch from outside.

Instructions to Class

- "Both players stand near the midline about 5 feet behind the short line. One player drops the ball to the floor and hits it to the front wall. The other player tries to return it to the front wall before it bounces twice on the floor. The rally continues until one player fails to return the ball. The other player then has scored 1 point. The player who did not score then starts the rally for the next point. Play continues until one player has scored 5 points."

Student Options

- "Do not count it as a trial until three shots have been hit to the front wall."
- "Increase or decrease the distance from the front wall."
- "Make up your own rules for scoring points."
- "Use your backhand only."

Student Success Goal

- Win two of three games

To Decrease Difficulty

- Allow players to play the ball after two bounces.
- Have player hit first shot to receiver's forehand.
- Play only one game.
- Hit ball softly.

To Increase Difficulty

- Points are scored only for balls hit into the backhand side of the court.
- Play more games.
- Allow full power on shots.

Step 4 **Beginner's Power Serve**

This serve is important for two reasons: Beginners need to learn serving rules, and it is a useful way to start games. You should demonstrate this serve several times to the class, covering both technique and rules. It also helps to demonstrate nonlegal serves such as short serve, long serve, three-wall serve, and ceiling serve. Use students and assistants to demonstrate if that helps.

Your first two or three demonstration serves should focus on where to drop the ball (relative to your body) and how to swing and direct the ball to the receiver's backhand, using principles from Step 2. Then three or four serves can focus on legal and nonlegal serves. Also serve a few to show the difference between serves that are faults and those that are outs. Have students refer to page 46 of *Racquetball: Steps to Success* (reproduced below as Figure 4.1) or to the American Amateur Racquetball Association (AARA) rule book when they want to review the faults and outs you've demonstrated.

Remember the saying "I hear and I forget, I see and I remember, I do and I understand." The sooner you let students serve and play, the sooner their understanding starts. Do not spend a lot of time now on improving technique. That will come later when you teach the power serve in Step 7.

One major objective for your students here should be to learn the difference between legal serves, faults, and outs. Another is to establish the habit of serving to the receiver's backhand. I recommend that you teach Steps 4 and 5 in the same lesson. Too much talk about faults and outs can be counterproductive. Your students will learn faster when they see faults and outs during drills.

At this stage, you should be observing and teaching proper wrist action, which generates power for the shot. Many students will develop this naturally, but a few will need help. Proper wrist action (on both forehand and backhand) first involves cocking the wrist on the backswing so the thumb points toward the ceiling. It then involves letting the racquet head pass the hand and wrist right after contact until the thumb again points toward the ceiling on the follow-through.

RETURN OF SERVES

The receiver should stand on the midline and about 6 or 8 feet from the back wall. Since you should teach Steps 4 and 5 together, your students will expect the serve to come to their backhand. Most beginners will want to start close to the back wall and to the backhand side of the midline. These are poor habits because they make returning the serve more difficult. You will have to remind your students many times about proper receiving position.

Teach your students to focus their eyes on the ball instead of the server's body movements. By doing so, they will have extra time to return the serve. If your students are having trouble get-

	Out	*Fault*
When does it happen?	Can occur on either first or second attempt.	Can occur on either first or second attempt.
What is the result?	No further attempt is allowed.	After first fault, one more is allowed. Two faults make an out.
How does it occur?	Any time service attempt does not strike front wall first.	Many types—all after service attempt has hit front wall first.
Special names or occurrences.	Whiff or miss, rebound hits server on fly, crotch serve.	Short, long, three-wall, ceiling.

Figure 4.1 Faults and outs on service attempts.

ting to the serve in time to return it, look for this error first.

Instructions for returning serves will be more meaningful if given just prior to the Serve-and-Return drill (see Drill 4).

STUDENT KEYS TO SUCCESS

- Use a forehand grip.
- Use a controlled swing.
- Keep eyes on ball.
- Recover after serve and move to center court.

Beginner's Power Serve Rating

CHECKPOINT	BEGINNING LEVEL	INTERMEDIATE LEVEL	ADVANCED LEVEL
Preparation	• Incorrect grip • Ball drop inconsistent	• Grip usually correct • Ball drop usually consistent	• Correct forehand grip • Ball drop consistently placed so it can easily be contacted at an angle that will direct the serve to opponent's backhand
Swing	• Usually starts too fast or too slow • Rushed • Arm and wrist stiff • Not much wrist action • No weight transfer	• Swing sometimes rushed • Usually smooth • Elbow sometimes leads • Some wrist action, but sometimes early or late • Weight transfer is early or late	• Smooth swing • Good timing • Wrist releases at contact • Good wrist action • Smooth weight transfer from back foot to front
Follow-Through	• Arm swing limited • Stands and watches serve	• Good arm swing • Usually moves to ready position after serve	• Full arm swing pulls hips and shoulders forward • Good extension • Moves easily and smoothly to ready position

Error Detection and Correction for the Beginner's Power Serve

This serve is easy for anyone who has played other racquet sports, but the player usually has to concentrate on the direction of the serve. Tennis players have to be told to let the wrist "snap," but usually pick that up right away. Beginners who have trouble with this serve need more fundamental work, such as hand-eye coordination. For these students, many of the earlier drills should be continued.

ERROR 🚫

CORRECTION

1. Student lacks power.

1. Encourage student to make a smooth swing with good wrist action. Hit the ball in the center of the strings. Power is not as important as control at this stage.

2. Student has trouble controlling direction of serve.

2. Make sure ball drop is in proper location: away from body and even with or forward of the front hip. Review with student the angle of the racquet face and ball direction [*Racquetball*, Step 2].

3. Serve hits side wall too soon and rebounds toward center of the court.

3. Tell student to move target away from corner or move starting position toward midline. Both corrections may be necessary. Perhaps tape targets to front wall.

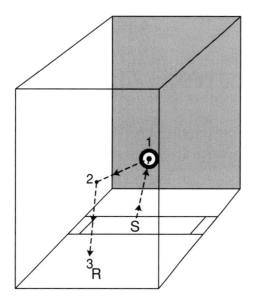

4. Student rushes swing, attempting to gain power.

4. Encourage student to focus on ball and try to make good contact. Power will come naturally.

ERROR   **CORRECTION**

5. Student forgets to return to center court after serve.

6. Receiver favors backhand side too much.

5. Have courtmate verbally remind partner after every serve. Put a square of tape on the center court area and ask server to touch area inside square after each serve.

6. Place an X on the floor on midline and 8 feet from back wall. Have player stand on the X to receive. Have receiver practice Drill 4.

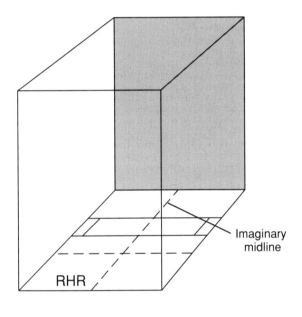

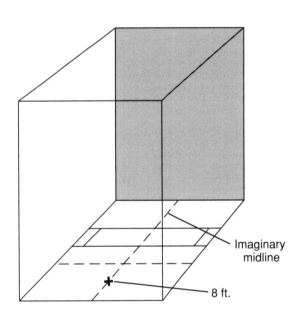

Beginner's Power Serve Drills

1. Ball Drop
[Corresponds to *Racquetball*, Step 4, Drill 1]

Group Management and Safety Tips

- Students can practice this drill anywhere and anytime.
- Only students having trouble should spend much time on this drill.
- Cover this drill once with the entire group.
- Spend only 1 or 2 minutes on this drill.

Instructions to Class

- "Find a spot on the court 4 or 5 feet from anyone else. Drop the ball 8 to 12 inches forward of your front hip and 8 to 12 inches to the side as if to serve. You should be able to catch the bounce without moving much. Drop the ball from your fingertips with the palm of your hand toward the floor. Do not throw it down or toss it away from your body. The ball should fall straight down and then bounce straight up."

Student Options

- "Set individual goals."
- "Practice on your own."

Student Success Goal

- 8 good drops out of 10

To Decrease Difficulty

- Reduce Success Goal to 5 out of 10.

To Increase Difficulty

- Increase Success Goal to 10 out of 10.

2. *Serve to Receiver's Backhand*
[Corresponds to *Racquetball*, Step 4, Drill 2]

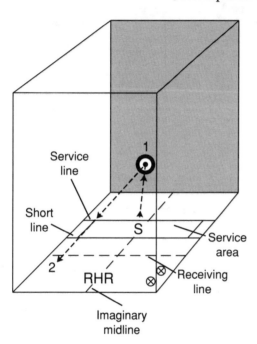

Service line

Short line

S

Service area

2

RHR

Receiving line

Imaginary midline

Group Management and Safety Tips

- Only one player can serve at a time.
- Other players can retrieve balls for server.
- Other players can observe and judge quality of serve.

Equipment

- 4 or 5 extra balls per court

Instructions to Class

- "Serve anywhere from the left side of the

midline inside the service area. Try to hit the serve to the backhand side of a right-handed receiver. Remember your ball must hit the front wall first and land behind the short line. Hit 10 serves to that side and then hit 10 to the backhand side of a left-handed receiver. Don't worry about power; just try for a legal serve."

Student Options

- "Set individual goals."
- "Have a contest within your group for the highest number of legal serves."
- "Take fewer attempts before exchanging turns with ball retrievers."

Student Success Goal

- 16 of 20 legal serves to backhand court (8 of 10 legal serves to right-handed receiver's backhand and 8 of 10 legal serves to left-handed receiver's backhand)

To Decrease Difficulty

- Decrease Success Goal.
- Count any legal serve in any location.

To Increase Difficulty

- Increase Success Goal.
- Count only serves that do not hit the side wall.
- Count only serves that bounce twice before reaching the back wall.

3. *Quality Serves to Backhand*
[Corresponds to *Racquetball*, Step 4, Drill 3]

Group Management and Safety Tips

- One player serves at a time.
- Other players can retrieve balls for server.
- Other players can observe and judge quality of serve.
- Remove any tape markers you use.

Equipment

- 4 or 5 balls per court
- One 2-foot by 2-foot cardboard box per court (to increase difficulty)
- Colored paper and tape (to decrease difficulty)

Instructions to Class

- "As you serve this time, you want to try to improve the quality of your serves. The better-quality serves are those that do not strike the side wall at all and that bounce twice before contacting the back wall. The quality is still acceptable if the serve strikes the side wall deep in the court or the back wall no higher than 2 feet. If the serve strikes the side wall, it should be within 10 feet of the back wall. In this drill your courtmates will judge the quality of your serves."

Student Options

- "Experiment with harder and softer serves and lower and higher targets on the front wall."
- "Change serving positions and observe the targets and angles required to place the serve in the corner."

Student Success Goals

- 5 quality serves out of 10 attempts to each corner
- 5 quality serves out of 10 attempts to cardboard box in each corner

To Decrease Difficulty

- Lower Success Goals.
- Place targets on front wall to help students direct serves.
- Count acceptable serves (any legal serve to the backhand side).

To Increase Difficulty

- Raise Success Goals.
- Place a 2-foot by 2-foot box in corner as target.

4. *Serve and Return*
[Corresponds to *Racquetball*, Step 4, Drill 4]

Group Management and Safety Tips

- Extra players must wait outside court.
- Extra players can keep score.
- Caution server never to look back at receiver after serving.
- Be sure students have been grouped by ability.
- Rotate extra players in after each game so they don't wait too long.

Instructions to Class

- "Play a serve-and-return game with a partner. The server gets 1 point for a serve to the receiver's backhand court. The receiver tries to return the serve to the front wall. The receiver gets 1 point for a legal return. The server does not try to play the return. The first player to score 7 points wins. Remember that only serves to the backhand side of the court count 1 point for the server. Switch server and receiver roles after each game. Play six games."

Student Options

- "Direct serves and returns to mentally targeted areas."
- "Give 2 points for legal returns."
- "Give a bonus point for an ace."
- "Allow server to serve to forehand occasionally if receiver is out of position."

Student Success Goal

- Win at least three of six games.

To Decrease Difficulty

- Allow 1 point for any legal serve, regardless of location.
- Reduce Success Goal.
- Do not keep score.
- Play fewer games.

To Increase Difficulty

- Receiver gets 2 points for successful return.
- Only an ace gets a point for the server.
- Receiver gets 2 points for any serve that can be returned with a forehand stroke.

Step 5 Strategy Rule #1— Hit It to Their Backhand

This is the first of six strategy rules that will help your students improve faster. Emphasize these rules as you teach them and look for situations to review them often with your students. Some of these rules have been adapted from David Belka's article, "Racquetballers: Put Yourself in the Driver's Seat" from the May 1983 *Journal of Physical Education, Recreation and Dance.*

Do not think this rule of hitting to the opponent's backhand is too obvious or too elementary for your students. Many will continue to hit the ball to their opponent's forehand—unaware—unless you continually remind them. This is why this rule is first: It is the most important and the most basic rule and must be first in the player's thoughts.

The rule should be taught in the same class period as Step 4. If your students direct the ball to the opponent's backhand when they begin to play, they will be better able to develop this strategy as a habit. It is easier and more efficient to develop good new habits than to break bad old ones.

Cover the rules quiz quickly and get your students into games as soon as possible. Encourage your students to discuss faults, outs, and violations among themselves while playing practice games. At first, they can replay a point and ask you about the rule later. Most questions will be about whether a serve was a fault or an out. You can generalize by saying, "Usually, if a serve does not hit the front wall first, it is an out." Reassure confused beginners that they will soon be able to tell the difference.

The most important thing at this stage is for students to play some games and get a feel for it while developing the habit of hitting shots to the backhand of their opponent.

Rules Quiz

1. When the server announces the score as 1-5, who is leading?
2. The server is struck by the ball while in the service area after the serve has bounced once. What is the ruling?
3. The receiver at center court returns the serve on the fly. What is the ruling?
4. The serve contacts the front wall, then the ceiling, then lands in front of the short serve line. Fault or out?
5. The serve contacts the front wall, then the ceiling, then lands behind the short serve line. Legal serve, fault, or out?
6. The server tosses the ball into the air (as in tennis) and serves an otherwise legal serve. Is this a legal serve?
7. The serve contacts the ceiling, then the front wall, then lands forward of the short serve line. Legal serve, fault, or out?
8. The serve contacts the front wall, then the back wall, then the floor behind the short serve line. Legal serve, fault, or out?
9. The server swings at a serve but misses. Retry, fault, or out?
10. The serve contacts the floor, then the front wall, then rebounds to land on the floor behind the short serve line. Legal serve, fault, or out?

Answers to Rules Quiz

1. Receiver.
2. Fault—short serve.
3. Illegal return—point for server: Receiver may not play the ball in front of the receiving line until it has bounced. (The answer is incorrect in the first printing of the participant's book. It has been corrected in all later printings. Check to see which printing your students have.)
4. Fault—as soon as it hits the ceiling.
5. Fault—as soon as it hits the ceiling.
6. No, the ball must bounce in the service area first. The server is out.
7. Out—the serve did not hit front wall first.
8. Fault—long serve.
9. Out.
10. Out—the serve did not hit the front wall first.

Calling Serves and Shot Placement Drills

1. *Legal Serve Decision Drill*
[New Drill]

Group Management and Safety Tips

- This can be done while retrieving balls for the server in some of the drills in Step 4.
- Set up a rotation so students have frequent turns at serving.

Instructions to Class

- "One person per court practices serves. Courtmates, in addition to retrieving balls for the server, call out 'legal,' 'fault,' or 'out' as soon as they can determine it."

Student Options

- "Take turns deciding status of the serve."
- "Keep track of most correct calls within your group."
- "Have a contest to see who can make the call the fastest."

- "Devise a point system for competition to see who can make the most correct calls. Include a penalty for incorrect calls."

Student Success Goal

- Make a correct call 80 percent of the time.

To Decrease Difficulty

- Lower Success Goal.
- Use participant's book to help you decide.
- Have rule book available.

To Increase Difficulty

- Increase Success Goal.
- Place a time limit (such as 5 seconds) upon decision.

2. *Hit to Their Backhand Drill*
[Corresponds to *Racquetball*, Step 5, Practice Game Drill]

Group Management and Safety Tips

- Students not playing should observe and score the game from outside the court.
- Make sure all scorers have a clear view into the court.
- Impress on scorers the need for accuracy.

Equipment

- Pencils, paper, clipboards

Instructions to Class

- "Go to your courts. Two people play a game to 7 points. The other courtmates take pencil and paper and keep track of how many shots one player hits to the opponent's backhand. Include serves. Also count the shots that go to their forehand. Divide the number of shots to the backhand by the total number of shots to calculate the percentage of shots hit to the opponent's backhand. Each observer scores just one player. Rotate so all get to play and have their shots charted."

Student Success Goal

- 75 percent of all shots to opponent's backhand

To Decrease Difficulty

- Decrease Success Goal.
- Have two observers for one player.
- Count serves only.

To Increase Difficulty

- Increase Success Goal.

Step 6   **Lob Serve**

Most beginning racquetball players tend to hit the ball as hard as they can all the time. Remind them that smarter players realize the importance of changing speeds and delivery. Slowing down the serve can aggravate aggressive opponents. As a teacher, you will also realize students will have better control if they don't swing so hard. Finally, the lob serve does not require a well-conditioned arm; the full power serve does. Using the lob serve (at least part of the time) might help prevent a sore arm or "tennis elbow" until players have time to condition their arms.

Most students will be surprised that the lob serve is harder to execute than it looks. It takes quite a while to learn to hit the soft stuff. But they will be pleasantly surprised how effective a properly executed lob serve is. Be sure to give your students the criteria for a quality serve and a good (or acceptable) serve:

- The quality down-the-line lob serve is close to the side wall but does not hit it. The serve bounces twice before contacting the back wall.
- The good (acceptable) down-the-line lob serve contacts the side wall not farther than 5 feet from the back wall. The serve may contact the back wall before the second bounce, but no higher than 3 feet.
- The quality cross-court lob serve strikes the side wall about 5 feet from back wall, then dies in a corner.
- The good (acceptable) cross-court lob serve contacts the side wall 5 to 10 feet in front of the back wall. It may contact the side wall a little higher than 5 feet but still forces the receiver to return the serve backhand.

These criteria will be used by the students to judge the quality of their courtmates' serves in drills presented in this and subsequent steps.

STUDENT KEYS TO SUCCESS

- Concentrate fully.
- Good ball bounce is essential.
- Swing smoothly.
- Open racquet face is vital.
- Touch and control are important.

Lob Serve Rating

CHECKPOINT	BEGINNING LEVEL	INTERMEDIATE LEVEL	ADVANCED LEVEL
Preparation	• Uses frying pan grip • Inconsistent ball bounce (does not bounce ball to the right and forward or does not bounce ball high enough) • Body rigid	• Uses forehand grip • More consistent — bounces ball so that contact on overhead stroke can be made with proper racquet angle • More relaxed	• Uses forehand grip • High bounce for overhead style serve and moves into good position • Knees, shoulders, and grip relaxed
Swing	• Arm stiff • Hits ball off center • Too hard or too soft • No hip or shoulder rotation	• Bends arm and uses wrist • Mostly sweet spot hits • Better control of velocity • Some rotation	• Good arm and wrist action • Makes good contact on the sweet spot • Good touch so that ball dies near back wall • Smooth rotation of hips and shoulders
Follow-Through	• Arm stops at contact • Weight doesn't transfer, remains on rear foot	• Arm continues through contact • Some transfer	• Arm and wrist action smooth and complete • Smooth transfer from rear foot to front

Error Detection and Correction for the Lob Serve

Bouncing the ball correctly is the biggest problem in learning the overhead stroke for the lob serve. Many students have not used their nondominant hand for this type of skill. The ball must be thrown downward with considerable force to bounce 3 to 4 feet higher than their racquet shoulder. Most can bounce it hard enough but not accurately enough, and those students need a lot of practice and encouragement to master the skill. You also can encour-age them to use the sidearm stroke instead of the overhead.

It is my pet opinion that you can serve a much more effective down-the-line lob serve with an overhead stroke. Sometimes only the highly skilled and highly motivated players want to develop this stroke, so don't force everyone to use this technique. Other errors can be corrected easily by practicing and observing results.

ERROR   **CORRECTION**

1. Server has to reach too far forward or arm motion appears restricted when using overhead stroke.

1. Server must move into proper position. Ball must be high enough (3 to 4 feet) in front of racquet shoulder. Practice ball bounce.

Maybe student could use underhand or side-arm motion. Demonstrate for student correct racquet angle.

2. Ball contacts side wall too soon and re-bounds toward midline.

2. Suggest that server move mental target on front wall more toward center of front wall or have student move his or her starting position nearer to the side wall.

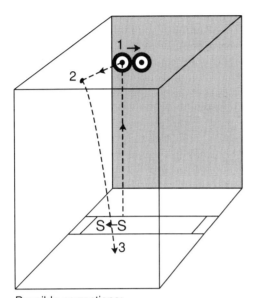

Possible corrections:
1. Move target away from side wall
2. Move starting position toward wall

3. Server doesn't get serve close enough to side wall.

3. Move starting position nearer to the side wall. Have server move mental target nearer the side wall.

Lob Serve Drills

1. *Phantom Lob Serve*
[New Drill]

Group Management and Safety Tips

- Three or four students can do this at the same time.
- Space students far enough apart to avoid racquet contact.
- Drill can be done in large group setting.

Instructions to Class

- "Find a spot in the service area. Practice an imaginary ball bounce and overhead lob serve with your racquet. Keep your racquet face open at the contact point to direct the ball high up on the front wall.

Try to visualize the ball and its path all through the swing. Now practice your side-arm lob serve in the same way."

Student Option

- "Work with your partners to help them with their form."

Student Success Goal

- 10 imaginary lob serves

To Decrease Difficulty

- Reduce the Success Goal.
- Go through movements in slow motion.

To Increase Difficulty

- Increase the Success Goal.

2. Ball Bounce

[Corresponds to *Racquetball*, Step 6, Drill 1]

Group Management and Safety Tips

- Drill can be done in a large group setting, usually before going to individual courts.
- Keep this drill short.
- You can note those having trouble for individual help later.
- This drill helps students correct the angle of a poor bounce.

Instructions to Class

- "Spread out to give yourself room to bounce the ball. Remember to bounce the ball hard enough so it bounces about 8 feet high, or 2 to 3 feet higher than your racquet shoulder. Let it bounce on the floor a second time. It should land just forward of your body about 8 to 12 inches and in front of your racquet shoulder. If the ball bounces too far away from you, try to figure out why."

Student Option

- "Practice this drill on your own in any setting."

Student Success Goal

- 7 good bounces out of 10

To Decrease Difficulty

- Reduce Success Goal.
- Allow student to practice in private without group distractions.
- Bounce ball with less force (4 or 5 feet high) to gain more control.

To Increase Difficulty

- Increase Success Goal.

3. Lob Serve (Down-the-Line) to Corner

[Corresponds to *Racquetball*, Step 6, Drill 2]

Group Management and Safety Tips

- Two servers can practice at the same time.
- Partners can retrieve balls for server.
- Develop a rotation schedule after the server has 10 serves so no one is waiting very long to take a turn at serving.

Equipment

- Two 2-foot by 2-foot cardboard boxes per court for targets (to increase difficulty)

Instructions to Class

- "Stand within 4 or 5 feet of the left side wall. Use either an overhand or a sidearm stroke. Your target on the front wall should be about 3 feet from the side wall and 4 feet from the ceiling. As it rebounds, the ball either should not hit the side wall at all or it should not hit until it is within 5 feet of the back wall. The ball should bounce twice before hitting the back wall or strike the back wall no higher than 3 feet before the second bounce. Work in pairs. One practices the lob serve while your partner notes the quality of the serve and retrieves balls for the server. A second pair can be practicing serves to the other back corner. Each person should serve 10 down-the-line lob serves to each corner and 10 cross-court lob serves to each corner."

Student Option

- "Compete for champion of the court."

Student Success Goal

- 6 quality serves of each 10 attempts to each corner from each serving position

To Decrease Difficulty

- Reduce Success Goal to 4.
- Count any serve that goes to the backhand side.

To Increase Difficulty

- Place cardboard boxes in corners for targets. A serve does not count unless it hits the box before the second bounce.
- Add 10 garbage lob attempts. [See *Racquetball*, Step 6, Drill 3.]

4. *Partner Return Lob Serve*

[Corresponds to *Racquetball*, Step 6, Drill 4]

Group Management and Safety Tips

- Server and receiver are the only two in the court.
- Caution students not to look back after serving.
- Other players wait outside court and can practice Drills 1 or 2.

Instructions to Class

- "The receiver assumes a position on the midline about 8 feet forward of the back wall and tries to return a lob serve to the backhand corner with any type of shot. Do not continue play. The receiver then gives the server feedback on the quality of the serve. The server must be sure never to look back, but to quickly assume a position at center court. Serve five serves, then exchange positions. Repeat once more. Rotate a new set of players into the court. Repeat the entire drill again with the server serving a garbage lob serve that hits front wall at a point halfway up to the ceiling and

rebounds with enough power to force the opponent to play the ball off a difficult shoulder-high bounce. Work in pairs in your court."

Student Options

- "Adapt the scoring system: 3 points for quality serve, 2 points for good serve, 1 for backhand side of court, 0 for any other."
- "Receiver competes with server by hitting more legal returns to the front wall than the server hits quality serves."

Student Success Goal

- Return 7 of 10 lob serves of each type

To Decrease Difficulty

- Reduce Success Goal.

To Increase Difficulty

- Increase Success Goal.
- Count only attempted returns of quality serves.

5. Lob Serve Game Situation

[Corresponds to *Racquetball*, Step 6, Drill 5]

Group Management and Safety Tips

- Two players play singles in the court.
- Others can be observers and chart quality and quantity of serves.
- Could use results of these games to move players to a new home court to equalize ability levels.
- Systematically rotate players in and out of the court so no one has to observe more than two games in a row.

Equipment

- Paper and pencils

Instructions to Class

- "Play a game to 7 points against someone from your court using regular singles rules. Use only lob serves. Play a second game against a different opponent. Give each other feedback about the quality of the serves after the game."

Student Option

- "Play each other for champion of the court."

Student Success Goal

- Play two games.

To Decrease Difficulty

- Play one game.
- Shorten games to 5 points.

To Increase Difficulty

- Play three or more games.
- Win two of three or three of five.

Step 7 **Power Serve**

Some of your students may not yet be able to execute a good power serve, but it's time to let the rest advance. The power serve is a refinement of the beginner's power serve and is the basic serve in racquetball. A helpful analogy is that serving is to racquetball what pitching is to baseball. This helps students grasp the importance of developing a good power serve.

As players understand the importance of staying low and hitting low power shots, you will see the level of their play quickly improve. Other players also will improve, but you will begin to see more and more differences in the range of abilities as the aggressive and agile players show spurts of improvement. (Now may be the time to regroup players by ability levels. Learning the game and having fun occur faster when players are evenly matched.)

The power serve intimidates some players, both in serving and receiving. Try not to let this

happen by keeping the players evenly matched and allowing timid players to keep using the beginner's power serve. Some will always want to play just for exercise and fun. Others will want the challenge of competing at the highest level they can find.

The exciting part of it for you as an instructor is that you can offer opportunities to beginners, intermediates, and advanced players within the same class.

STUDENT KEYS TO SUCCESS

- Drop the ball low.
- Move into shot with good weight transfer from front foot to back foot and to front again.
- Use smooth, controlled, powerful swings.
- Keep the body low.

Power Serve Rating

CHECKPOINT	BEGINNING LEVEL	INTERMEDIATE LEVEL	ADVANCED LEVEL
Preparation	• Bounces ball too high	• Bounces ball lower	• Drops ball low (6 to 10 inches) and out in front (2 feet) of body
	• Has trouble with footwork	• Can use good footwork, but sometimes must think about it	• Uses smooth footwork and weight transfer (see Figure 7.1)
	• Cannot keep body low while moving	• Can keep body lower than before with effort	• Can move smoothly while keeping body low

Power Serve Rating

CHECKPOINT	BEGINNING LEVEL	INTERMEDIATE LEVEL	ADVANCED LEVEL
Swing	• Same as beginner's power serve • Sidearm swing makes angle of racquet face inconsistent • Very little sense of timing • No shoulder and hip rotation and faces front wall and swings with arm only • Inconsistent or little weight transfer	• Usually swings too hard and too fast • Sidearm swing with racquet face inconsistent • Has trouble with timing of swing and release • Some rotation but usually jerky • Jerky transfer sometimes too quickly or too much to front foot	• Swings with good power and timing • Sidearm and underhand swing with good angle of racquet face • Directs ball to backhand side of receiver • Smooth swing, good timing, good wrist action • Complete hip and shoulder rotation (rotates from facing side wall at contact) • Smooth transfer from rear foot to front foot and maintains good balance
Follow-Through	• Arm movement is jerky and incomplete	• Usually overemphasized arm movement	• Arm comes across body smoothly

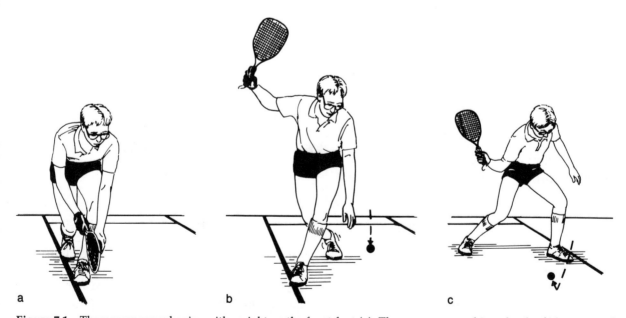

a   b   c

Figure 7.1   The power serve begins with weight on the front foot (a). The server moves his or her back foot toward the front wall, shifting weight to that foot (b), then steps into the ball, transferring weight again to the front foot (c).

Error Detection and Correction for the Power Serve

There are many possible errors in attempting the low, hard power serve. Probably the biggest error is for students to rush their movements when attempting to generate power. Emphasize that smooth body movements and good contact with the ball will generate the desired power, and that placement is more important than sheer power. Also tell the students that the ball appears to be traveling much faster to a person trying to return the ball than to the server who hit it.

ERROR

CORRECTION

1. Student rushes movements.

1. Remind student that power comes only with good timing and contact. Emphasize control over power.

2. Body stays too high while moving through the service motion.

2. Have student take smaller steps. Emphasize bending knees.

3. Student has trouble with timing of footwork, swing, and weight transfer.

3. Practice the footwork and swing drill without the ball. (See Drill 1.) Later, when the ball is added, have students concentrate on dropping the ball. Then footwork and swing will start automatically at the right time.

ERROR 🚫   **CORRECTION**

4. Server has little or no shoulder and hip rotation.

4. Have student check feet before serving. Toes should be pointed toward side wall. Have student keep nonracquet shoulder pointed toward the front wall until the hitting action starts, then rotate the hips and shoulders with the swing. Front foot should open up and toes point to front wall when stepping.

5. Receiver is too close to back wall.

5. Tell student to touch wall with racquet and arm outstretched, then take two steps toward front wall. Could also mark this spot with tape on the floor.

6. Receiver is too far to backhand side of imaginary midline.

6. Remind student to straddle midline. Mark midline with tape on floor.

Power Serve Drills

1. *Footwork*
[Corresponds to *Racquetball*, Step 7, Drill 1]

Group Management and Safety Tips

- This can be a group drill if room is available.
- It's helpful to use the service area.
- A demonstration is very helpful. Either do it yourself or have an experienced student demonstrate for you.
- After demonstration, students can go to their home courts for practice.

Instructions to Class

- "Practice your footwork and swing without a ball. Remember you can step on the service line but not over it. Start slowly and accelerate into the ball. Remember, first the weight is all on your front foot. Next, your rear foot moves toward the front wall. You drop the ball and all your weight transfers to the back foot. You step forward with your front foot and your weight transfers with it as you strike the ball nice and low. Your back foot comes forward toward the front wall as you're following through so you can square up and get ready to return to the center court position."

Student Options

- "Work with a partner to help improve your footwork."
- "Practice on your own while you are waiting for a court."

Student Success Goal

- 20 times done properly

To Decrease Difficulty

- Have student complete steps in slow motion.
- Reduce Success Goal.

To Increase Difficulty

- Increase Success Goal.
- Can add ball drop to the footwork drill. [See *Racquetball*, Step 7, Drill 2.]

2. *Power Serve to Back Left- and Right-Hand Corners*
[Corresponds to *Racquetball*, Step 7, Drills 3 and 4]

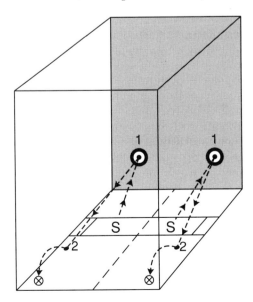

Group Management and Safety Tips

- Two servers can practice at the same time, one to each corner.
- Courtmates can retrieve balls.
- Utilize targets on walls. Mark a 2-foot square about 3 feet high and 4 feet away from the corner (to increase difficulty).
- Placement of targets on wall depends on starting position of server.
- Courtmates can comment on the quality of the serves.
- Remove targets from wall after class.

Equipment

- Colored tape to mark targets on front wall (to increase difficulty)

- Medium-sized (about 2 feet by 2 feet) cardboard box per court (to increase difficulty)

Instructions to Class

- "Try 10 power serves to the left back corner. The quality serve will not hit the side wall and will bounce twice before reaching the back wall. The acceptable serve may hit the side wall deep in the court within 5 feet of the back wall or may hit the back wall no higher than 3 feet. Rotate with your retriever. Repeat the drill, practicing some serves to the right rear corner because you may face a left-handed receiver."

Student Options

- "Set individual goals."
- "Vary the angle of the serve by starting from different locations."
- "Use targets on the front wall to aim your serve."

- "Make mental targets on the floor to determine starting location."

Student Success Goal

- 5 out of 10 serves are quality serves to each side

To Decrease Difficulty

- Decrease the Success Goal.
- Count both acceptable and quality serves.
- Count any serve to the backhand side of the court.

To Increase Difficulty

- Increase Success Goal.
- Put a 2-foot by 2-foot cardboard box in rear corner and count only serves that hit the box.
- Put targets on the front wall with tape and count only serves that hit targets.

3. *Return of Power Serve*
[Corresponds to *Racquetball*, Step 7, Drill 5]

Group Management and Safety Tips

- Only server and receiver can be in the court.
- This is a good drill for someone who has trouble returning serves. It can be used later on an individual basis as needed.
- Remind server not to look back toward receiver after serve.

Instructions to Class

- "Pair off two to a court. Courtmates can do Drill 1 or other drills outside while waiting for their turn."
- "One person serves trying for quality serves. Receiver tries to return each serve to the front wall. Receiver gets 1 point for every serve returned. Server gets 1 point for every legal serve not returned. First player to score 5 points wins this game. Then exchange positions for another game. Trade off with your courtmates until each person has played four games, two as server and

two as receiver. The server is allowed to serve to the forehand if the receiver is playing out of position."

Student Options

- "Subtract points for serves that are faults or outs."
- "Serve a set number of serves (5 or 10). The person with most points after that is the winner."

Student Success Goal

- Win at least half of the games played.

To Decrease Difficulty

- Allow 2 points for each return of serve.
- Do not keep score.

To Increase Difficulty

- Try to win three of four games.
- Server gets points for quality serves only.

4. *Power Serve Game*
[New Drill]

Group Management and Safety Tips

- Two players to a court.
- Remind servers not to look back.
- Remind players of all safety rules, especially wearing goggles.
- You can use results to move players to new home courts.
- Courtmates can observe games and discuss rules and situations while waiting their turns.

Instructions to Class

- "Play a game to 5 points using regular rules except that the server must use power serves only. After A and B finish, C and D will play. When C and D finish, the losers will play. Finally, the winners will play. If time remains, play someone in your group you have not played."

Student Options

- "Play only other students you wish to play. You can decline if you recognize that you would not be competitive."
- "Play other players on adjacent courts if time allows."
- "Earn a bonus point for an ace."

Student Success Goal

- Win at least half of games.

To Decrease Difficulty

- Reduce Success Goal.
- Disregard win-loss record.

To Increase Difficulty

- Increase Success Goal.

5. *One-Serve Game*
[New Drill]

Group Management and Safety Tips

- This is good for teaching players to concentrate on making a good serve.
- Limit to two players to a court.
- Remind servers not to look back.
- Courtmates can observe games and discuss rules and situations while waiting their turns.

Instructions to Class

- "Using your power serve, play a game to 5 points. Use the regular playing rules with this exception: The server gets only one attempt at each point; that is, an out or a fault will retire the server immediately. This will put a little more pressure on the server, but should help you concentrate on making a good serve. Play everyone in your court."

Student Options

- "Use any degree of power you desire."
- "Award a bonus point for an ace."

Student Success Goal

- Win at least half of games.

To Decrease Difficulty

- The server may use the beginner's power serve to be more competitive.

To Increase Difficulty

- Not applicable

Step 8   Strategy Rule #2— I Own Center Court

Have some fun with your students when talking about this rule. Ask them to repeat the rule to themselves, then ask them to say it out loud. Most will be a little embarrassed and will repeat it softly. You can ask them to say it with conviction or do so yourself. The whole class is likely to break into smiles, which gives you an opportunity to discuss the importance of being aggressive in occupying the center court position. The person who can monopolize center court has control and will most likely win the rally. Tell them that owning center court is the first step to being able to hit passing shots and kill shots, two rally-ending shots that you will introduce in Steps 9 and 12.

TRAIN YOUR STUDENTS TO MOVE TO THE CENTER

This is one of the two major principles of Rule #2. Players must develop the habit of moving quickly toward center court each time they make a shot. Some will do this naturally; others will

have a great deal of trouble remembering to move. It is one thing to understand the principle and another to remember to move each time.

DEVELOP SHOTS THAT WILL MOVE YOUR OPPONENT OUT OF CENTER COURT

This is the second principle of Rule #2. If your opponent is in center court, you cannot occupy it unless you move the opponent out. That is why Steps 9 and 10 (Passing Shots and Ceiling Shots) follow this rule and may be taught in conjunction with this rule. It helps to reinforce a strategy if you give students the tools to apply that strategy. It also helps give purpose to learning the two shots and when to apply them. It is very meaningful if you can teach at least one of the shots (passing shots or ceiling shots) in the same class period. Referring to Rule #2 when you talk about these defensive shots is very helpful.

Center Court Drills

1. *Wall Touch*

[Corresponds to *Racquetball*, Step 8, Drill 1]

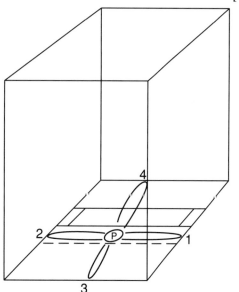

Group Management and Safety Tips

- Limit to one person on each court.
- Courtmates can watch and offer encouragement.
- Courtmates should stand near corners to be out of the way.
- Courtmates can time the runner.

Equipment

- 1 stopwatch per court (to increase difficulty)

Instructions to Class

- "This drill has two purposes. One is to help you practice your footwork and agility. The other is to help you train yourself to move back to center court. Start in the ready position at center court. Run and touch the right side wall with your racquet. Return to the ready position at center court. Then run and touch the left side wall and return. Next, turn and run toward the back wall, keeping your eyes on the front wall. Touch the back wall and return to center court in the ready position. Run to touch the front wall. Cross over and run back to center court while watching the front wall over your shoulder. Set up at center court. Repeat the complete sequence two more times."

Student Options

- "Vary the pace."
- "Experiment with shuffle step and cross-over step when running to side walls."

- "Memorize the number of steps to center court position from walls."
- "Have a timed contest between students."

Student Success Goal

- 3 repetitions of touching walls and returning to ready position at center court

To Decrease Difficulty

- Decrease the Success Goal.
- Decrease the pace.

To Increase Difficulty

- Increase the Success Goal.
- Increase the pace.
- Time students with a stopwatch. Students will be interested in improving their times.

2. *"Simon Says"*
[Corresponds to *Racquetball*, Step 8, Drill 2]

Group Management and Safety Tips

- Two people play per court.
- Other courtmates stand near corners.
- Remove tape after use.

Equipment

- 1 stopwatch per court (Student Options)
- Colored tape to mark target areas (Student Options)

Instructions to Class

- "This drill is to help you develop your re-action time. It also can be a lot of fun. Set up at center court in the ready position. Your partner will call 'right, left, front, or back.' When your partner calls out, go to that wall, take a swing at an imaginary ball, and return as fast as you can to a ready position at center court. Be prepared to go to any of the four walls each time. When you have done this six times, exchange with your partner."

Student Options

- "Vary the pace."
- "Have someone time you in each direction."
- "Give the next command before the player gets to center court."
- "Mark a target area near each wall. The player must get to that spot before swinging."

Student Success Goal

- 6 repetitions

To Decrease Difficulty

- Decrease the Success Goal.
- Decrease the pace.

To Increase Difficulty

- Increase Success Goal.
- Increase the pace.

3. X Marks the Spot

[Corresponds to *Racquetball*, Step 8, Drill 3]

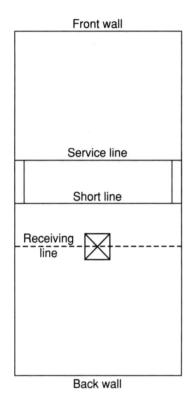

Front wall

Service line

Short line

Receiving line

Back wall

5 feet behind short line on the imaginary midline.)
- Paper and pencils to keep score

Instructions to Class

- "Your court has an X marked inside a square in the center court position. Play a game using regular rules except for scoring of points. The only way to score a point is to touch the X (or the square) with your foot during play. Exchange serves as in a regular game but remember that either server or receiver can score points in this game. You can also score more than 1 point during a rally by touching the X after each shot. First player to 15 points wins."

Student Options

- "Play a game with regular scoring rules. Touching the X adds a bonus point each time."
- "Play a game as above, but give 2 bonus points for each time X is touched."

Student Success Goal

- Win at least three of five games.

To Decrease Difficulty

- Decrease the Success Goal.
- Award 2 or 3 points for each return to X.
- Decrease length of each game to 7 or 10 points.

To Increase Difficulty

- Increase the Success Goal to seven of nine games.
- Increase length of each game to 20 or 25 points.

Group Management and Safety Tips

- Limit to two players per court.
- Courtmates keep score from outside court.
- Set up a rotation system so that students are not keeping score for more than two games in a row.
- Remove tape after use.

Equipment

- Colored tape to mark X on floor. (Actually make the X inside a 3-foot by 3-foot square

4. I Own Center Court

[Corresponds to *Racquetball*, Step 8, Drill 4]

Group Management and Safety Tips

- Limit to two players per court.
- Observers can watch from above or outside courts.
- Rotate players so no student observes more than two games in a row.

- Copy Return to Center Court Chart before class.

Equipment

- Paper and pencils
- Appropriate number of charts

Instructions to Class

- "Play a game to 7 points. Have an observer count the number of shots you hit, including serves. Also have the observer count the number of times you return to center court after each shot. The winner is the person who returns to center court the highest percentage of times."

Student Option

- "Have a contest with others in your group."

Student Success Goals

- Return to center court 90 percent of the time.

- Return to center court more often than your opponent.

To Decrease Difficulty

- Decrease Success Goal to 75 percent or 80 percent.
- Play games to 5 points.

To Increase Difficulty

- Increase Success Goal to 95 percent or 100 percent.
- Play games to 11 or 13 points.

Return to Center Court Chart

Date: _____

Player: _____   Observer: _____

Directions: Observe one player in a _____-point game. For each shot the player hits (including serves), mark an "X" through the appropriate number below. If the player returns to center court after making the shot, circle the shot number you just X'd. If the player fails to return to center court, do not circle the shot number. After the game, figure the player's return to center court percentage using the formula provided.

Game 1:

1	2	3	4	5	6	7	8	9	10	11	12	13	14	15	16	17	18	19	20
21	22	23	24	25	26	27	28	29	30	31	32	33	34	35	36	37	38	39	40
41	42	43	44	45	46	47	48	49	50	51	52	53	54	55	56	57	58	59	60

$$\frac{\text{number of circles}}{\text{number of "X"s}} \times 100 = \text{_____} \% \text{ of the time player returns to center court}$$

Game 2:

1	2	3	4	5	6	7	8	9	10	11	12	13	14	15	16	17	18	19	20
21	22	23	24	25	26	27	28	29	30	31	32	33	34	35	36	37	38	39	40
41	42	43	44	45	46	47	48	49	50	51	52	53	54	55	56	57	58	59	60

$$\frac{\text{number of circles}}{\text{number of "X"s}} \times 100 = \text{_____} \% \text{ of the time player returns to center court}$$

Game 3:

1	2	3	4	5	6	7	8	9	10	11	12	13	14	15	16	17	18	19	20
21	22	23	24	25	26	27	28	29	30	31	32	33	34	35	36	37	38	39	40
41	42	43	44	45	46	47	48	49	50	51	52	53	54	55	56	57	58	59	60

$$\frac{\text{number of circles}}{\text{number of "X"s}} \times 100 = \text{_____} \% \text{ of the time player returns to center court}$$

Step 9   **Passing Shots**

The passing shot is the most basic of all the shots in racquetball. It can be used offensively—as a rally-ending shot—or defensively—to force your opponent to vacate center court. Students usually pick up the latter concept easily, but two aspects often cause them problems. The first is that beginners usually hit passing shots so high and hard it is easy for their opponents to play the ball off the back wall. So, you must remind students to target their shots lower on the front wall and hit the ball softer and challenge them to get the ball to bounce twice before it reaches the back wall.

The second problem occurs on down-the-line pass attempts. If the ball hits the front wall too close to the corner, it will contact the side wall and rebound toward the midline. This makes it easy for the opponent to play the ball. Often this problem arises because the player is swinging too hard and loses accuracy.

It would confuse your students to cover at the start of the lesson all passing shots and which to use in which game situation. When you introduce each shot and set up a drill for it, give students an idea of when to use it; emphasize the proper defensive use of the passing shot. After your students have practiced both cross-court and down-the-line passes, go into detail about game situations covered in the participant's book. Review this after players have learned all the shots. At that time you will want to emphasize the proper offensive use of the passing shot as well.

STUDENT KEYS TO SUCCESS

- Check position of opponent.
- Visualize a target on front wall no higher than 3 feet.
- Use controlled swing.

Passing Shot Rating

CHECKPOINT	BEGINNING LEVEL	INTERMEDIATE LEVEL	ADVANCED LEVEL
Preparation	• Hits ball before locating opponent • No apparent plan • Position of opponent not considered	• Locates opponent • Sometimes plans shots • Sometimes forgets position of opponent	• Good setup and knows where opponent is • Takes time to decide which shot to use • Proper shot for opponent's position
Execution	• Swings too hard • Ball hits too high on front wall	• Attempts to control swing • Ball sometimes hits too high on front wall	• Smooth swing with power controlled • Ball hits 3 feet high or lower on front wall
Result	• Ball hits side wall on down-the-line pass • Ball is too high • Ball easily playable off back wall	• Ball hits side wall deep in court on down-the-line pass • Shots are usually low • Ball is usually playable off the back wall	• Ball flys near side wall, but does not hit it on down-the-line pass • Shots are low enough • Ball bounces twice before hitting back wall

Error Detection and Correction for Passing Shots

Trying to determine what a player is thinking is difficult. You can ask after the fact, but the teachable moment is usually gone. But you can see the physical aspects. Often, poor passing shots are a result of poor body mechanics. For instance, it is hard to control the racquet when facing the front wall. Look for that as a first check in detecting errors. Later, you can help your students select the appropriate passing shot for the particular situation.

ERROR 🚫

CORRECTION

1. Player faces front wall while making shot.

2. Player contacts ball too high and too soon.

3. Ball hits side wall and rebounds toward midline.

4. Opponent can easily play ball off back wall.

5. Student attempts wrong type of passing shot.

1. Explain that arm movement is restricted by body. Review proper form. Videotape student. Ask student to review Steps 2 and 3.

2. Have student check position of opponent before hitting shot. Tell student to wait for ball to drop.

3. Have student check body position. Tell student to visualize a target on wall and to swing at one half to three fourths power and concentrate on accuracy.

4. Have student use less power. Lower target on front wall. Try to make ball bounce twice before reaching the back wall.

5. Discuss situation with student and set up situations for student to see logical selection. Have student do Drill 4 (Decision Time) and Drill 6 (The Passing Game).

Passing Shot Drills

1. *Down-the-Line Passes*
[Corresponds to *Racquetball*, Step 9, Drill 1]

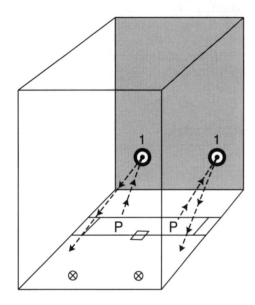

service area on the imaginary midline to make this drill more realistic. A person standing there with outstretched arms would be even better. Hit a down-the-line pass, trying to keep the ball from hitting the side wall. Keep the ball in play for as many consecutive down-the-line passing shots as possible. Others can retrieve balls. One person drills on forehand passing shots, and another on backhand passing shots."

Student Option

- "Time yourself to see how many you can do in 30 seconds."

Student Success Goals

- 8 consecutive forehand down-the-line passes
- 6 consecutive backhand down-the-line passes

To Decrease Difficulty

- Decrease Success Goals.
- Move closer to front wall (in front of the service line).
- Move toward midline.

To Increase Difficulty

- Increase Success Goals.
- Attempt shots from deeper in the court (3-5 feet behind short line).
- Move closer to side wall.

Group Management and Safety Tips

- All players can be in courts at once.
- One can drill with forehand, and one with backhand.
- Others retrieve balls and observe drill.
- Note that the drill in *Racquetball: Steps to Success* has goals for deeper positions.

Equipment

- Box, chair, or other similar object, 1 per court

Instructions to Class

- "One person stands near the side wall in the service area. Place a box or chair in the

2. Partner Down-the-Line Passes

[Corresponds to *Racquetball*, Step 9, Drill 2]

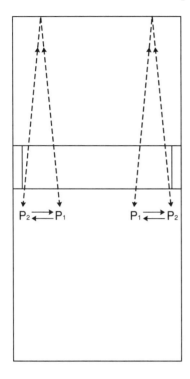

Group Management and Safety Tips

- Two people play per court for beginning and intermediate players.
- Advanced players may use both sides of the court at the same time if they choose. Do not have players return to center court if two teams are using the court at the same time.
- Remove tape after use.

Equipment

- Use colored tape for marking center court, as in Step 8, Drill 3, X Marks the Spot (Stu-

dent Option). Place X inside 3-foot by 3-foot square 5 feet behind the short line on the midline.

Instructions to Class

- "With a partner, alternate hitting down-the-line passing shots. Keep the ball in play as long as possible. Stay on the forehand side and near the center court area. If a shot touches the side wall, it ends the drill. Next, repeat the drill on the backhand side."

Student Options

- "Make a contest of the drill. Partners, try to hit more consecutive passes than another team of courtmates."
- "Mark center court and return there after every shot."

Student Success Goals

- 12 consecutive forehand down-the-line passing shots
- 8 consecutive backhand down-the-line passing shots

To Decrease Difficulty

- Decrease Success Goals.
- Move nearer to front wall.
- Allow shots to contact side wall.

To Increase Difficulty

- Increase Success Goals.
- Do drill on backhand side of court.
- Move farther from front wall.

3. Partner Cross-Court Pass
[Corresponds to *Racquetball*, Step 9, Drill 4]

Group Management and Safety Tip

- Two people play per court.

Equipment

- 1 box, chair, or other similar object per court

Instructions to Class

- "With a partner, stand in center court near opposite walls. Hit cross-court passes to each other, one partner hitting forehand shots, other hitting backhands. Continue until one player misses or hits a poor shot. Then change places and repeat the drill. Place a box, chair, or courtmate on the midline near the short line to help you visualize the angle necessary to pass someone."

Student Options

- "Form two-person teams to compete with courtmates."

- "Compete against your partner: 2 points for a good backhand pass, 1 point for a good forehand pass."

Student Success Goal

- 20 consecutive cross-court passes (after each has done the drill both ways)

To Decrease Difficulty

- Decrease Success Goal.
- Decrease distance from front wall.

To Increase Difficulty

- Increase Success Goal.
- Increase distance from front wall.

4. Decision Time
[Corresponds to *Racquetball*, Step 9, Drill 6]

Group Management and Safety Tips

- Limit to two players on a court at one time.
- Courtmates can observe and discuss the decision while waiting their turn.
- Players can study their options as outlined in Step 9 of the participant's book while waiting.
- Rotate so no one has to observe more than two games in a row.

Instructions to Class

- "This drill can help you decide which passing shot to use in a game. Player A starts the rally with an easy shot to the front wall. Player B returns it with another easy shot that comes back near the center of the court. Player A then hits another easy return and yells, "Now!" Player A then takes a position near the midline or either side wall. Player B should try to pass player A with the appropriate passing shot. [Review *Racquetball*, Step 9, Figures 9.1 through 9.4.] Player A tries to return the passing shot. Do not continue the rally. Player B gets 1 point for a successful pass. Player A gets 1 point for returning the attempted pass. The

first player to get 5 points wins the game. Then rotate and exchange roles. Play six games. Remember, when your opponent is in the middle of the court and in front of you always use the cross-court pass. When your opponent is near the wall and you are near the center, go down the line along the opposite wall. When you and your opponent are near center court and your opponent is at the imaginary midline, you can choose either down the line or cross-court."

Student Success Goal

- Win four out of six games.

To Decrease Difficulty

- Decrease the Success Goal.
- Play each game to 3 points.
- Player A can take an exaggerated position so the best shot is very obvious.

To Increase Difficulty

- Increase the Success Goal.
- Let player A disguise his position until the last moment.
- Give player A 2 points for returning an attempted pass.

5. *Monster Drill*
[New Drill]

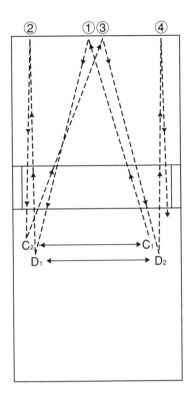

Group Management and Safety Tips

- Caution players to watch for each other while moving.
- This is for advanced players; it is too difficult for poor or average players.
- You should demonstrate the drill by having two players walk through the movements without hitting a ball.

Equipment

- Chalkboard and chalk to diagram paths of shots and players

Instructions to Class

- "This drill will enable one person to work on down-the-line passes, and the partner to work on cross-court passes. We will walk through it first without hitting the ball. The cross-court player begins near the right side wall (C1) and as deep as the center court position. He or she hits a cross-court pass to the left side wall where the down-the-line player is waiting (D1). The cross-court player moves to the left side wall (C2) to receive the shot from the down-the-line player. After hitting a down-the-line pass, the down-the-line player moves to the right side wall (D2) to return the cross-court player's second shot. The down-the-line player's second shot stays near the right side wall. The cross-court player returns to his or her original position to return the down-the-line player's second shot. The down-the-line player returns to his or her original position to return the third shot from the cross-court player. Continue this sequence until one player misses. Then exchange roles."

Student Options

- "Set up at center court before continuing on to next receiving position."
- "Use a box, chair, or other object in the service area on the midline to help visualize opponent."
- "Use the drill as competition. First one to miss loses the game."

Student Success Goal

- 16 consecutive shots (4 complete cycles) without losing control of the ball

To Decrease Difficulty

- Reduce the Success Goal.
- Players hit soft shots.
- Allow players to play ball on any bounce.

To Increase Difficulty

- Increase the Success Goal.
- Players try for successful passing shots.

6. *The Passing Game*

[Corresponds to *Racquetball*, Step 9, Drill 7]

Group Management and Safety Tips

- Two people play per court.
- This is also a rather advanced drill, but not quite as difficult as Monster Drill.
- Rotate in waiting players so no one has to sit out more than two games.

Instructions to Class

- "Play a game of racquetball with a partner. Change the rules so that you alternate serves regardless of who wins the rally. You may use any shots you wish but only a quality passing shot scores a point. Remember that a quality passing shot is one that does not touch the side wall and bounces twice before reaching the back wall. If the rally ends any other way, the server and receiver exchange roles but no point is scored. Play the passing game to 5 points."

Student Options

- "Play regular rules, but give a bonus point if the winning shot is a quality passing shot."
- "Play regular rules, but use only passing shots."
- "Play to more than 5 points."

Student Success Goal

- Win three of five games.

To Decrease Difficulty

- Allow any type or quality of passing shot to score a point.
- Score 2 points for a passing shot.
- Lower game to 2 or 3 points.

To Increase Difficulty

- Increase number of points required to win the game.
- Exchange serves only after a successful passing shot.
- Only passing shots by server score points.

Step 10 Ceiling Shots

Teach your students that the ceiling shot, if learned well, can get an opponent out of center court and can keep him or her off balance while you wait for a weak return that gives you an opening for an offensive shot. A ceiling shot also can disrupt the game of an impatient power player. Veteran players know that it is primarily a defensive shot, but it can end the rally for many beginning players who do not have the skill to return it.

Most beginning racquetball players don't use the ceiling shot often enough. If you can motivate them to use this shot, they will see how effective it is and use it more. This shot and the passing shot should be taught as the two basic shots to make your opponent vacate the center court position.

STUDENT KEYS TO SUCCESS

- Get into position quickly (hit forehand if possible).
- Focus eyes on ball.
- Take ball high and in front of player.
- Reach up and out to hit.
- Shift weight into shot.
- Smooth stroke at three-fourths power.
- Hit ceiling 2 to 5 feet from front wall.

Ceiling Shot Rating

CHECKPOINT	BEGINNING LEVEL	INTERMEDIATE LEVEL	ADVANCED LEVEL
Preparation	• Slow moving into position • Poor body position and takes ball too high or low and positions self too far forward or back • Does not face side wall • Does not take racquet back behind shoulder • Dominant foot often in front for forehand • Weight seldom transferred to back foot	• Usually arrives in time • Adequate body position and usually proper relationship to ball • Sometimes faces side wall • Back swing too limited and hurried • Dominant foot in back for forehand • Weight usually transferred to back foot	• Gets there early • Good body position and under ball • Usually faces side wall • Full back swing, elbow bent and wrist cocked • Dominant foot back for forehand with weight firmly on back foot • Weight firmly on back foot

Ceiling Shot Rating

CHECKPOINT	BEGINNING LEVEL	INTERMEDIATE LEVEL	ADVANCED LEVEL
Execution	• Often misses or mishits balls • Lacks power, so ball does not get deep enough • Not enough weight shift into shot	• Hits ceiling too far from or too near front wall • Often hits ball too hard and ball comes off back wall too far • Weight shift sometimes too early or late	• Well-directed ball hits ceiling near front wall for proper angle • Uses half to three-fourths of power and ball dies in backcourt • Smooth weight shift with good timing
Follow-Through	• Wrist is stiff • Arm swing stops at contact • Recovers balance slowly	• Wrist release is limited • More complete arm swing • Recovers balance quickly	• Good wrist action with thumb pointing down for forehand and toward back of hand for backhand • Arm swings forward and down across body for forehand and across body for backhand • Recovers balance and starts to move immediately toward center court

Error Detection and Correction for the Ceiling Shots

The most common error in hitting ceiling shots is failing to get good position on the ball. Practicing the shots in drills will teach most players good positioning easily and quickly, especially for the forehand shot. The backhand ceiling shot is much more difficult. Returning a backhand ceiling shot to your opponent's backhand requires excellent positioning, racquet control, and power. Tell your students to be patient with themselves. This skill will increase as their competition level rises. Usually the level of their competition is such that they don't have to hit perfect or high-quality shots to be effective.

ERROR   **CORRECTION**

1. Student has poor body position for forehand ceiling shot. Lets ball get too far back.

1. Tell student to get under the ball as if to catch it with dominant hand. This is the position from which the student will want to hit the shot.

2. Student can't return backhand ceiling shots to backhand side.

2. Usually poor body position and closed racquet face directs ball to center of court. To correct this, have student face side wall and contact ball closer to rear shoulder.

ERROR 🚫

CORRECTION

3. Student doesn't get deep enough to get good ball position. Return often hits ceiling too far from the front wall and doesn't rebound against the front wall.

3. Tell student to (a) turn back to the front wall and run toward the back wall, (b) watch the ball over shoulder, and (c) get there quickly to have enough time to plant the back foot and shift weight from rear foot to front while hitting the ball. (See Drill 2.)

a

b   c

4. Student has trouble determining where the ball should contact the ceiling and/or front wall to get the proper depth on shot.

4. Give student advice on targets. Tell student that this target changes depending upon position in the court. Have student practice Drill 3.

Ceiling Shot Drills

1. *Phantom Ball*
[Corresponds to *Racquetball*, Step 10, Drill 1]

Group Management and Safety Tips

- Can do drill in any large open space.
- Can have 10 to 12 students in one court.
- Space students so they can swing safely.
- Students can practice on their own.
- Drill can identify students who might need extra help.
- Spend only a few minutes on this drill.

Equipment

- Racquets only (no balls)

Instructions to Class

- "Imagine that you are hitting a ceiling shot. Say to yourself, 'Look up, push off back foot, swing.' As you look up, transfer your weight to your back foot. Push hard as you start to swing. Transfer your weight to your front foot as you complete your swing."

Student Option

- "Experiment with different amounts of weight transfer."

Student Success Goal

- 50 phantom swings for both forehand and backhand

To Decrease Difficulty

- Reduce the Success Goal.

To Increase Difficulty

- Increase the Success Goal.
- Have student run back to set up before phantom swing.

2. *Setup Drill*
[New Drill]

Group Management and Safety Tips

- Can do drill in any large area, but it works best in racquetball court.
- Courtmates can help each other with signal, timing, and critique.

Equipment

- Racquets only (no balls)
- 1 stopwatch per court (to increase difficulty)

Instructions to Class

- "Set up in a ready position at center court. When partner says 'go,' turn and run to the back court. Stop quickly and set up as if to return a ceiling shot with another ceiling shot. Remember to push hard with your rear foot while swinging at the imaginary ball. Alternate forehand and backhand strokes. Swing toward an imaginary ceiling target about 4 to 6 feet back from the front wall."

Student Option

- "Do on your own without commands."

Student Success Goal

- 25 setups with each stroke

To Decrease Difficulty

- Do at a slower pace.
- Reduce the Success Goal.

To Increase Difficulty

- Time students with a stopwatch to motivate them to increase speed of setup.
- Increase the Success Goal.

3. *Bounce-and-Hit Ceiling Shots*
[Corresponds to *Racquetball*, Step 10, Drill 2]

Group Management and Safety Tips

- One player hits shots in each court.
- Others can retrieve balls and feed hitter.
- One player can score and/or critique hitter.
- Rotate from retriever to scorer to hitter.

Equipment

- 1 cardboard box (about 2 feet by 2 feet) per court (To Increase Difficulty)

Instructions to Class

- "From near the center court position, bounce the ball hard on the floor or toss it up into the air. Get into position quickly and execute a ceiling shot. Hit it toward the backhand corner of a right-handed player. Aim for the ceiling about 5 feet from the front wall. Hit 10 shots, then try to hit 10 more to the other corner."

Student Options

- "Experiment with different targets and different locations on the floor."
- "Try to hit backhand ceiling shots also."
- "Hit front wall ceiling shots also."

Student Success Goal

- 8 of 10 good ceiling shots to each corner

To Decrease Difficulty

- Teacher or partner can bounce or toss ball.
- Reduce the Success Goal.

To Increase Difficulty

- Require shots to be near side wall without contacting it.
- Add a target (such as a 2-foot by 2-foot cardboard box) in the corner. [Corresponds to *Racquetball*, Step 10, Drill 3.]
- Require student to hit shots with backhand stroke.

4. *Ceiling Shot Rally*
[Corresponds to *Racquetball*, Step 10, Drill 4]

Group Management and Safety Tips

- Limit to one player in a court.
- Other courtmates observe from outside.
- This makes an excellent warm-up.

Instructions to Class

- "Start in midcourt or the back court. Hit a ceiling shot and then try to return it with another ceiling shot. Hit as many consecutive ceiling shots as you can. If you get to eight, consider yourself an expert and try some other options."

Student Options

- "Try to direct all shots to your forehand side using a forehand stroke."
- "Try to direct all shots to your backhand side using a backhand stroke."
- "Alternate forehand ceiling shots and backhand ceiling shots."
- "Try to have some of your ceiling shots hit the front wall first."
- "Do this drill with a partner, alternating shots."

Student Success Goal

- 8 consecutive ceiling shots

To Decrease Difficulty

- Lower the Success Goal.

To Increase Difficulty

- Make up a specific sequence of shots.
- Increase the Success Goal.

5. *Partner Ceiling Shot Rally*

[Corresponds to *Racquetball*, Step 10, Drill 5]

Group Management and Safety Tips

- Limit to two players on a court.
- This is an advanced drill, especially the backhand corner option.
- Other players observe outside and wait for their turn to rotate in.

Instructions to Class

- "This is a partner drill. One player starts with a ceiling shot. The other player returns it with a ceiling shot. Keep the ball near the midline. You may use the regular ceiling shot or the reverse (front wall first) ceiling shot. This drill will help you improve your ceiling shots. It is also a good warm-up before a game."
- "Next, try to hit your ceiling shots to the opposite corner each time. You probably wouldn't do this in a game, especially to your opponent's forehand. However, it is a good drill for learning the correct angles."
- "Finally, try to keep a rally going using ceiling shots only to your partner's backhand corner. This is very difficult but will make you a better racquetball player."

Student Options

- "Make a contest out of any one or all three options."
- "Compete with your courtmate to see who misses first."
- "Count your total score and compare to another team of two players."
- "Add a third player and take every third shot."

Student Success Goals

- 12 consecutive ceiling shots near midline
- 8 consecutive ceiling shots to alternate corners
- 6 consecutive ceiling shots to backhand corner

To Decrease Difficulty

- Hit forehand to forehand only.
- Decrease the Success Goals.

To Increase Difficulty

- Increase the Success Goals.
- Try to make every other shot a reverse ceiling shot.

6. *Ceiling Shot Game*

[New Drill]

Group Management and Safety Tips

- Two players compete per court.
- This drill will magnify the differences in skill levels.
- Use this as a tournament to move players to a higher ability court (move-up tournament).
- This drill will motivate students to use ceiling shots in all games.

Instructions to Class

- "In this game, the only way to score a point is by hitting a ceiling shot that your opponent cannot return. You win or keep the serve any other time your opponent makes an error, but those do not score points. Follow all other regular racquetball rules. Play a game to 7 points and then rotate courtmates."

Student Options

- "Compete with courtmates for champion of court."
- "Add a third person and return every third shot."

Student Success Goal

- Win two of three games.

To Decrease Difficulty

- Decrease the Success Goal.
- Play games to fewer points.

To Increase Difficulty

- Points are scored only while serving.
- Increase the Success Goal.
- Play games to more points.

Step 11 Strategy Rule #3—Love the Back Wall

When students learn to let the ball go to the back wall, they are on the way to becoming complete racquetball players. Some do this easily and naturally. Others can't seem to learn the angles or develop confidence to let the ball go past them. Encourage your students to let the ball go to the back wall, even though they will make lots of frustrating mistakes. Help them play through the frustration and try to reduce the pressure on them to win rallies and games during this period. It will pay great dividends later, though they might lose rallies and points while learning the angles and back wall play.

Providing your students both guidelines and encouragement will help them learn back wall play faster. Remind them that when judging the carom off the back wall, the angle of the rebound off the back wall typically equals the angle of approach, and be sure to refer often to the four principles described on page 90 of *Racquetball: Steps to Success* when encouraging your students. That is,

1. Always keep your eye on the ball. Never let your back turn to the ball or let it go behind you. If you must turn to follow the ball, pivot like a basketball player.
2. Don't chase the ball—go to meet it. Estimate where it will be and go to that spot quickly so you will have time to make any final adjustments to the ball. (See Figures 11.1 and 11.2.)
3. As you turn and move, stay away from the walls and out of the corners. Most initial movement should be close to the imaginary midline.
4. Wait for the ball to drop. How far you let it drop depends on the shot you want to make.

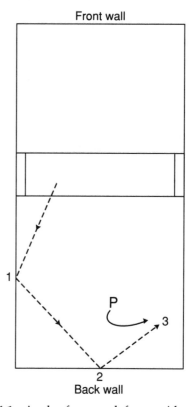

Figure 11.1 Angle of approach from a side wall to the back wall causes the ball to rebound at a greater angle off the back wall.

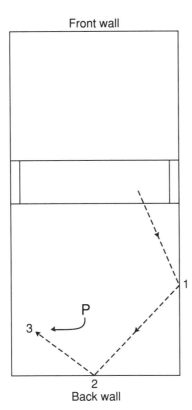

Front wall

P

3

1

2

Back wall

Figure 11.2 Side wall to the back wall angled rebound to a right-handed player's backhand.

STUDENT KEYS TO SUCCESS
- Turn with ball.
- Keep eyes fixed on ball.
- Don't chase ball; go to meet it.
- Stay near midline as you turn and move.
- Wait for ball to drop while planning shot.

Back Wall Rating

CHECKPOINT	BEGINNING LEVEL	INTERMEDIATE LEVEL	ADVANCED LEVEL
Preparation	• Seldom lets ball go to back wall	• Lets high balls go to back wall • Sometimes lets ball go to back wall when not playable	• Makes good decisions
Execution	• Often out of position and chases ball but can't catch up • Has to hit ball with poor body mechanics • Returns are not planned	• Has to make last-minute adjustment to ball • Sometimes must rush shot • Sometimes remembers opponent's position	• Has good position and lets ball come to him or her • Lets ball drop low (usually below knees) • Plans appropriate shot
Follow-Through	• Disoriented	• Recovers slowly or not at all	• Recovers and moves to center court in ready position

Error Detection and Correction for Back Wall Play

Learning the angles off the back wall comes easily to some and hard to others. Remind students that the rebound angle is usually equal to the approach angle (except when the ball is spinning, i.e., has "English" on it). Errors in playing the back wall usually fall into one of three categories:

1. Not letting the ball go to the back wall when it should,
2. being out of position to play the rebound from the back wall, or
3. letting the ball go to the back wall when it shouldn't.

All three types of errors can be corrected with experience. Remove the pressure to win points and games to encourage students to learn back wall play. Try to notice when the frustration level is high and explain that everyone can learn back wall play, that it just takes longer for some. Remind students of the four principles and encourage them to do lots of drills.

ERROR   **CORRECTION**

1. Student does not let ball go to back wall when appropriate.

1. Encourage student to let more balls go to back wall. Have student play nonscoring games and then occasionally just observe the bounce off the back wall instead of trying to play it. Also have student practice Drill 2, Back Wall Setup.

2. Student too close or too far away to make a good, smooth return.

2. Emphasize to student to calculate where the ball will go and then set up an arm's length plus a racquet's length away to avoid being in the same place as the ball. Practice Drill 1, Back Wall Toss.

3. Student cannot judge angled returns. Student usually is chasing the ball to try to get into position to hit it.

3. Tell student not to get discouraged. This is a difficult shot, and some pick it up faster than others. Review the four principles. Encourage student to do Drill 4, Chase the Rabbit.

Back Wall Drills

1. *Back Wall Toss*

[Corresponds to *Racquetball*, Step 11, Drill 1]

Group Management and Safety Tips

- Two students can practice at the same time in one court.
- One can work on forehand, other on backhand.
- Remind students to be aware of courtmate while practicing.
- Others can retrieve balls.
- This is one of the best drills to learn back wall play.

Instructions to Class

- "Stand about 5 or 6 feet from the back wall. Toss the ball against the back wall about 3 or 4 feet high. Let it bounce once and then return it to the front wall with a forehand stroke. You may have to move quickly to get into proper position to make a good shot. Remember to push hard off your back foot so you get the proper weight transfer. When you have hit 25 forehands, rotate with your courtmates. When everyone has finished hitting forehands, repeat the drill using your backhand stroke."

Student Options

- "Throw ball so it hits floor first and then the back wall. Try to play the return before it bounces on the floor."
- "Play ball on any bounce."

Student Success Goals

- 25 forehand returns to front wall
- 25 backhand returns to front wall

To Decrease Difficulty

- Play ball after two or three bounces.
- Reduce the Success Goals.
- Have partner toss ball.

To Increase Difficulty

- Increase the Success Goals.
- Have partner toss ball and vary the speed of rebound.
- Play the ball off the back wall before it strikes the floor.

2. *Back Wall Setup*

[Corresponds to *Racquetball*, Step 11, Drill 2]

Group Management and Safety Tips

- Only one player plays per court.
- This is a good drill if you have extra courts and extra players.
- This makes a very good warm-up drill.

Instructions to Class

- "From the middle of the court, stroke the ball to the front wall high enough and hard enough that it will bounce once on the floor and then bounce off the back wall. Get into position so you can return the ball to the front wall before it again bounces on the floor. Do this 10 times and then set yourself up for 10 backhand returns."

Student Options

- "Vary your starting positions."
- "Vary the power of your shots."

Student Success Goals

- 7 successful forehand returns of 10 good setups
- 7 successful backhand returns of 10 good setups

To Decrease Difficulty

- Reduce Success Goals.
- Have partner hit the setups.
- Have partner throw the ball to back wall.

To Increase Difficulty

- Increase Success Goals.
- Plan and execute a ceiling shot or passing shot that comes off the back wall.

3. *Continuous Back Wall Setup*

[Corresponds to *Racquetball*, Step 11, Drill 3]

Group Management and Safety Tips

- Only one player plays per court.
- This is a good warm-up activity.
- This is a good activity if you have an odd number of players and an extra court.

Instructions to Class

- "Try to keep the ball continuously in play off the back wall by hitting your returns so they come off the back wall. Use either forehand or backhand strokes as necessary. Then try it using only forehand strokes. Finally, try the drill using only backhand strokes."

Student Option

- "Vary the force of your shots to change the difficulty of the return."

Student Success Goals

- 10 continuous returns (any stroke)
- 7 forehand returns (forehand only)
- 5 backhand returns (backhand only)

To Decrease Difficulty

- Reduce Success Goals.

To Increase Difficulty

- Increase Success Goals.

4. *Chase the Rabbit*

[Corresponds to *Racquetball*, Step 11, Drill 4]

Group Management and Safety Tips

- One player plays in court at a time.
- This makes a good warm-up activity.
- This makes a good activity if you have an odd number of players and an extra court.

Instructions to Class

- "Hit a shot to the front wall from the center court position. Run to return the ball after any number of bounces. Try to hit the shot high and hard enough so it will get to the back wall on one or two bounces. Don't worry if you can't get to the ball before the second bounce. Just return it whenever you can get to it, but try to play it before it crosses the short line on its way to the front wall after rebounding from the back wall. Sometimes, hit the ball so it strikes the side wall after coming off the front wall. This will give you some angled returns off the back wall so you can learn how to return them."

Student Options

- "Make up your own version."

- "Play the ball after three bounces every time."
- "Play the ball after two bounces every time."

Student Success Goal

- 5 minutes chasing the rabbit

To Decrease Difficulty

- Reduce time to 3 or 4 minutes.

To Increase Difficulty

- Increase time to 6 or 7 minutes.

5. *Partner Pass*

[Corresponds to *Racquetball*, Step 11, Drill 5]

Front wall

- Review the four principles of back wall play.

Instructions to Class

- "Player A sets up in center court position. From nearby, player B drops and strokes a cross-court passing shot. B makes the ball hit the side wall high and hard enough to get an angled rebound from the back wall. A attempts to return the ball before it bounces twice. Alternate positions after five attempts. Then repeat the drill, forcing the returner to use a backhand stroke."

Student Options

- "Use only forehand returns."
- "Use only backhand returns."
- "Hit a pass from behind a player so he or she doesn't know when or where the shot is coming from."

Student Success Goal

- 6 of 10 playable shots returned

To Decrease Difficulty

- Reduce Success Goal.

To Increase Difficulty

- Increase number of trials.
- Increase the Success Goal.

Group Management and Safety Tips

- Two players play on a court.
- This drill requires intermediate or advanced skill level.

6. *Partner Continuous Back Wall Setup*
[Corresponds to *Racquetball*, Step 11, Drill 6]

Group Management and Safety Tips

- Two players play on a court.
- Drill requires intermediate or advanced skill level.

Instructions to Class

- "Partners, set each other up off the back wall. Mix straight front-to-back returns with angled returns as desired. Keep the ball high enough so it can be played off the back wall."

Student Options

- "Add ceiling shots and passing shots."

- "Make this drill into a game, either cooperative or competitive."

Student Success Goal

- 10 continuous back wall returns

To Decrease Difficulty

- Reduce the Success Goal.
- Allow returner two bounces.

To Increase Difficulty

- Increase the Success Goal.
- Require all backhand returns.

7. *The Back Wall Game*
[Corresponds to *Racquetball*, Step 11, Drill 7]

Group Management and Safety Tips

- Two players play on a court.
- This drill requires intermediate or advanced skill level.

Instructions to Class

- "In this game, the only way to score a point is to return a shot off the back wall that your opponent cannot return. Start each rally with a serve. Alternate serves regardless of who loses the rally or who wins a point. Hit passing shots and ceiling shots off the wall to win the rally and score a point. Know where your opponent is and plan what shot to hit. Move with your shot, then move quickly toward center court and anticipate a return. Don't look back. The first player to 7 points wins."

Student Option

- "Add other conditions to scoring a point, such as requiring two shots after the serve before attempting to score."

Student Success Goal

- Win two out of three games

To Decrease Difficulty

- Decrease the Success Goal.
- Play games to fewer than 7 points.

To Increase Difficulty

- Increase the Success Goal.
- Play games to more than 7 points.

Step 12 Kill Shots

By now your students should be getting better, their rallies are probably lasting longer, and they are enjoying the game more. The more alert and aggressive players have discovered that hitting the ball low gives good results, but others are still just hitting the ball to the front wall and waiting for their opponent to make a mistake and lose the rally. This is the ideal time to talk about using kill shots as offensive tactics to win a rally.

The kill shots are both the most difficult to master and most difficult to practice. The conditions that call for a kill shot during a game are easy to talk about but hard to set up in drills. To use a kill shot, one should be in the center court area and in front of the opponent. If the opponent has been driven deep to the back wall, from which he or she is likely to have trouble recovering rapidly, the conditions are ideal. These tactical conditions can occur only during a game, but they should be demonstrated while students practice kill shots so they can better understand their use. The various kill shots should be demonstrated and practiced one at a time so stu-

dents don't get confused and unable to focus on the fundamentals and the target. Demonstrate one (straight wall kill first) and then send them to practice. Call them back to discuss and demonstrate the pinch kill, the inside corner kill, and the drop (or volley) kill, sending them to practice after each demonstration.

Emphasize that the approach angle equals the rebound angle. This helps students realize they must wait for the ball to drop low before striking it. Another point that must be emphasized is that the shot does not have to be hit hard, but that it must be hit low. Point out the standard for a quality kill shot: the ball must bounce two times before rebounding back to the service line.

STUDENT KEYS TO SUCCESS

- Wait for ball to drop low.
- Try to position for a forehand.
- Achieve a good body position; stay low.
- Move with the shot.
- Use a smooth, powerful swing.

Kill Shot Rating

CHECKPOINT	BEGINNING LEVEL	INTERMEDIATE LEVEL	ADVANCED LEVEL
Preparation	• Does not wait for ball to drop low • Slow in positioning	• Waits for ball to drop lower than knees • Gets to ball just in time	• Moves while waiting for ball to drop as low as ankle height • Good footwork and has time to swing smoothly

Kill Shot Rating

CHECKPOINT	BEGINNING LEVEL	INTERMEDIATE LEVEL	ADVANCED LEVEL
Execution	• Misses ball often	• Rushes swing	• Sidearm controlled swing for forehand kill and good timing on backhand swing
	• Balance problem makes it hard to stay low	• Swings too hard and body comes up on swing	• Good balance allows body to stay low
	• Ball hits too high on front wall	• Ball hits too low at times	• Ball stays low (2 to 6 inches high) on front or side wall
	• No weight transfer	• Some weight transfer	• Good weight transfer
	• Faces front wall	• Usually faces side wall	• Front shoulder toward target
	• Does not think about shot	• Sometimes makes incorrect judgments about which kill shot to hit	• Shows good shot selection: Uses straight (front wall) kills to go down the line away from the opponent or if opponent is in the backcourt and nearer one of the walls, will hit a pinch kill or an inside corner kill to that corner
Follow-Through	• Head and eyes move too soon	• Some head movement during swing	• Head and eyes still and focused on ball
	• Stands and watches shot	• Recovers quickly	• Moves quickly to center court

Error Detection and Correction for Kill Shots

As with earlier shots, the biggest problem to overcome here is to teach your students not to swing too hard. Even for a kill shot, control is much more important than power. Beginners also need to develop the confidence and sense of timing it takes to allow the ball to drop low before hitting it. A physics description can help:

Explain that the approach angle and the return angle are identical so the ball must approach the wall nearly parallel to the floor if it is to rebound low with the potential to win a point. Understanding these two problem areas will help your students correct many technique errors.

ERROR 🚫

CORRECTION

1. Student contacts ball too high.

1. Explain angles of approach and return. Have student practice swing without ball, keeping arm low and parallel to floor. Suggest Drill 1, Paper Cup Kill drill.

2. Position while making shot is incorrect. Body is not low enough or faces front wall.

2. Tell student to continue to adjust position while waiting for ball to drop. Use Paper Cup Kill drill.

3. Inconsistent results: some too high, some too low.

3. This is probably because of improper weight transfer. Tell the student to start behind the ball, catch up to it, and bend sideways on forehand shots. Work on timing on backhand shots.

ERROR 🚫   CORRECTION

4. Student lacks power on shots.

4. Probably due to lack of shoulder and hip rotation. Have student (a) turn toward back corner on back swing; (b) hit through the ball; and (c) "pose for picture" at end of follow-through. Check for good weight transfer.

5. Student rushes body movements and arm swing.

5. Tell student to relax and try to move in slow motion. Suggest Paper Cup Kill drill in slow motion.

Kill Shot Drills

1. *Paper Cup Kill*

[Corresponds to *Racquetball*, Step 12, Drill 1]

Group Management and Safety Tips

- All players can be on court at once.
- One drills while others retrieve balls.
- Others can critique form while waiting their turns.

Equipment

- 8 to 10 paper cups 4 to 8 inches tall per court

Instructions to Class

- "Place the ball on a paper cup near the imaginary midline and the short line. Start 3 or 4 feet behind the ball and attempt a kill shot. Remember to stay low, shift your weight from back to front, and don't swing too hard. Practice your straight kill and your corner kills (the pinch and the inside corner). Practice both your forehand and backhand strokes. Remember, quality kill shots must bounce twice before crossing the service line."

Student Option

- "Attempt kills only from optimum angles such as opposite side wall from corners."

Student Success Goal

- 5 effective kill shots of each type using both forehand and backhand strokes

To Decrease Difficulty

- Use a taller cup.
- Set goal at number of attempts instead of effective kill shots.

To Increase Difficulty

- Increase the Success Goal.
- Subtract one from total for every ineffective attempt.

2. *Kill From Midcourt*

[Corresponds to *Racquetball*, Step 12, Drill 2]

Group Management and Safety Tips

- One player attempts kill.
- Other students retrieve balls and judge form.
- You can use cups/cans for targets on front wall.
- Players rotate duties.

Equipment

- 8 to 10 cups per court for holding ball and 4 to 6 cups or 2 cans per court for targets (Student Option)

Instructions to Class

- "Standing deep in center court, toss the ball out in front of you. Move into the ball and hit kill shots with your forehand. Try to stay low and move with your stroke. Hit straight, pinch, and inside corner kills. Next, try the same procedure using your backhand."

Student Options

- "Try to determine best angles, shots, and corners depending upon your position."
- "You can use targets (cups or cans)."
- "Courtmate can toss ball for attempt."

Student Success Goal

- 5 effective kill shots of each type using both forehand and backhand

To Decrease Difficulty

- Set goal at number of attempts rather than effective kill shots.
- Use only forehand stroke.
- Let ball bounce more than once.

To Increase Difficulty

- Increase the Success Goal.
- Subtract one for every ineffective attempt.
- Attempt from deeper in court.

3. *Kill Setup*
[New Drill]

Group Management and Safety Tips

- This can be done in pairs or alone.
- Others must wait outside court.

Instructions to Class

- "One person hits a ball to the front wall hard enough and high enough that the other player can try to hit a kill shot off the back wall. The player attempting the kill shot should start from center court position. After five setups, exchange roles. Next, try setting up your partner with ceiling shots hit so they rebound to center court. Remember to let the ball drop low when attempting this kill shot."

Student Options

- "Add other types of shots to try to kill."

- "Continue playing out the rally."
- "Choose the type of kill that is appropriate."

Student Success Goal

- 5 quality kill shots from each type of setup

To Decrease Difficulty

- Reduce the Success Goal.
- Set goal at five attempts rather than at five quality kills.
- Reduce quality of kill shot.

To Increase Difficulty

- Increase the Success Goal.
- Setup person gives more difficult attempts: deeper in court, etc.

4. *Partner Kill*
[Corresponds to *Racquetball*, Step 12, Drill 5]

Group Management and Safety Tips

- Two players play per court.
- This is a good drill to work on return of kill shots.

Instructions to Class

- "Two players to a court. Rally the ball against the wall hard enough so that it comes off the back wall. After at least three hits, you can attempt a kill. Partner attempts to rekill. Next, try the same procedure with a ceiling-shot rally."

Student Option

- "Make a scoring game out of the drill."

Student Success Goal

- 5 of 10 kill shots from back wall or ceiling shot that cannot be returned

To Decrease Difficulty

- Attempt kill at any time.
- Reduce the Success Goal.
- Partner tries to give easier shot to kill.

To Increase Difficulty

- Increase the Success Goal.
- Kill shots must bounce twice before crossing service line.
- Partner tries to give difficult shot to kill.

5. Drop (Volley) Kill Game

[New Drill]

Group Management and Safety Tips

- Two players play per court.
- Others can work on other drills in extra courts, or be rotated in.

Instructions to Class

- "Play a game to 5 points using regular playing rules. Try to move your opponent up and back with different shots. While your opponent is back, use a surprise drop kill shot. Count 1 point for this attempt. Count 2 additional points if it is a quality drop kill."

Student Options

- "Combine this game with a 5-point kill game."
- "Vary the rules so a successful drop kill wins the game regardless of the score."

- "Vary the number of points for an attempt and a quality drop kill."

Student Success Goal

- Win two of three games

To Decrease Difficulty

- Decrease the Success Goal.
- Decrease quality of drop kill to include any that opponent fails to return.
- Decrease number of points required to win game.

To Increase Difficulty

- Increase the Success Goal.
- Increase number of points required to win game.

6. Five-Point Kill Game

[Corresponds to *Racquetball*, Step 12, Drill 6]

Group Management and Safety Tips

- This drill/game is played with two players.
- You can add a third player and use cutthroat (Step 14) rules.

Instructions to Class

- "Play a game to 5 points using regular playing rules with the following modifications. Each player hits shots trying to gain the center court position. Each looks for a kill opportunity. Any type of kill shot may be attempted. Only kill shots will score points. This is true for both receiver and server. Errors or other shots during play can end the rally or cause change of serve, but will not score a point."

Student Options

- "Decide on the quality of the kill shot required to score a point."

- "Decide that kill shots attempted while behind opponent cannot score a point."
- "Play to more or fewer points."
- "Play with regular scoring rules but give a bonus point for kill shots."

Student Success Goal

- Win two of three games

To Decrease Difficulty

- Decrease number of points or number of games.
- Decrease quality of kill shots required to win a point.

To Increase Difficulty

- Increase the Success Goal.
- Increase number of points required to win game.
- Only kill shots by server score points.

Step 13   Strategy Rule #4— Stay Out of the Detour Zone

The previous three strategy rules are the most basic: They relate to the way the game should be learned. Rules in this and the next two steps will help your students improve the quality of their shots and strategy.

Beginners usually return shots to the front wall without much thought about shot quality or where the ball will rebound. This rule should teach them that their shot quality is important and will affect the strength of their opponent's return.

The detour zone should be described to your students as the area inside a 3- or 4-foot border around the outside of the front wall.

It helps to mark the zone. Plastic colored tape is expensive but an option. Colored chalk is inexpensive but defies drawing a straight line. Best may be carpenter's chalk string. Any hardware store would stock this, and a salesperson could explain how to "snap a line." The chalk can be removed easily with a damp cloth.

Urge your students to get to the ball early so they have adequate time to set up for a good shot. Also tell them to let the ball drop low before hitting passes and kill shots and to use this time to locate the opponent and plan their shot. They should discover that better shots will result in weaker returns from their opponent. Remind them often of this fact.

STUDENT KEYS TO SUCCESS

- Get in position early.
- Wait for ball to drop.
- Locate opponent.
- Plan shot.
- Visualize target within border.

Stay Out of the Detour Zone Rating			
CHECKPOINT	**BEGINNING LEVEL**	**INTERMEDIATE LEVEL**	**ADVANCED LEVEL**
Preparation	• Rushes return • Unaware of opponent's position	• Uses Rule #4 usually • Usually locates opponent's position	• Arrives early and plans shot • Aware of opponent's position
Execution	• No apparent target	• Usually aware of detour zone	• Has target in mind: always within border and outside detour zone
Results	• Few shots in border	• Some shots in border	• Most shots in border • Shot is low or near side wall

Error Detection and Correction for Stay Out of the Detour Zone

Most errors on this topic are mental. Be patient with your students because everyone goes through the stage of just returning the ball to the front wall without planning the shot or taking time to make a quality shot. Constantly remind students to plan quality shots, but also realize they must play a lot before they are secure enough to let the ball drop before they hit and place it. Returning high shots into the detour zone is not usually as much a problem as low shots into the detour zone.

ERROR ⊘

CORRECTION

ERROR	CORRECTION
1. Player hits many shots into detour zone without realizing it.	1. Have student chart other students as in Drill 3. The realization that many shots are hit into the detour zone must come before student improves shot quality.
2. Student rushes return without letting ball drop.	2. Ask student to try to contact ball below knee level, except for ceiling shots and Z-shots (Step 17).
3. Student realizes fault but cannot seem to correct it.	3. Mark court with tapes or lines. Have student play or practice in marked court. (Refer to Drills 1 and 2.)

1. Avoid the Detour Zone
[Corresponds to *Racquetball*, Step 13, Drill 1]

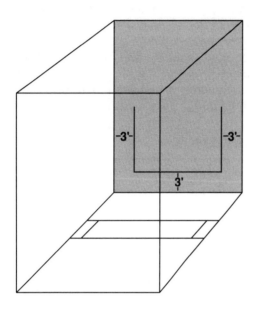

Group Management and Safety Tips

- Two players play on a court.
- Courtmates can observe from outside and give feedback on quality of shots.
- Detour zone must be marked before class.
- You may want to make a larger or smaller zone depending on students' abilities.
- Erase all wall marks after class.

Equipment

- Chalk, colored tape, or carpenter's chalk line (to mark zone before class)
- Step ladder, if possible (to mark zone before class)

Instructions to Class

- "With a partner, warm up using some of the shots and drills you have learned. Try to keep your shots out of the marked detour zone, or inside your 3-foot border. Even after you have warmed up, remember that accuracy is more important than power. If you have trouble keeping your shots out of the detour zone, hit the ball with less power and concentrate on accuracy."

Student Option

- "Mentally change the size of the border."
- "Practice shots alone."

Student Success Goal

- 5 minutes of practice hitting shots

To Decrease Difficulty

- Decrease the Success Goal.
- Increase the size of the border (decrease the detour zone) before class starts.

To Increase Difficulty

- Increase the Success Goal.
- Decrease the size of the border (increase the detour zone) before class starts.

2. Detour Zone Game

[Corresponds to *Racquetball*, Step 13, Drill 2]

Group Management and Safety Tips

- Two players play on a court.
- Detour zone must be marked before class.
- You may want to make a larger or smaller zone depending on students' abilities.
- Remove zone markings after class.

Equipment

- Colored chalk, colored tape, or carpenter's chalk line (to mark detour zone)
- Step ladder, if possible (to mark detour zone)

Instructions to Class

- "Using a court marked with a 3-foot border, play a game to 5 points. Use regular rules with two exceptions. First, only winning shots hit into the border score a point. Alternate the serve as in a regular game, but remember the server might not receive a point for holding the serve. Second, winning shots hit by the receiver can score a point as well as those hit by the server."

Student Options

- "Mentally change the size of the border."
- "Change the rules so only a server's winning shots inside border count as points."
- "Play a tournament among courtmates for champion of the court."

Student Success Goal

- Win two out of three games to 5 points

To Decrease Difficulty

- Increase size of border before class starts.
- Play a game to 2 or 3 points.
- Decrease the Success Goal.

To Increase Difficulty

- Decrease size of border before class starts.
- Increase the Success Goal.
- Play games to 10 points or more.

3. Detour Zone Chart

[Corresponds to *Racquetball*, Step 13, Drill 3]

Group Management and Safety Tips

- At least three players play per court, two to play and one or two to chart.
- Reproduce detour zone shot chart ahead of time for student use.

Equipment

- Pencils
- Detour zone charts

Instructions to Class

- "Play a game to 7 points. Ask a classmate to chart your shots using the detour zone chart. The observer marks an X where every shot hits the front wall. The X is circled if the shot ends the rally. When the game is over, calculate the percentage of shots that hit in the high zone, low zone, side zones, and detour zone. Analyze the results to see if you are using the right kind of shots and to see if the quality of the shots is high."

Student Options

- "Mentally change the size of the border."
- "Limit point-winning shots to selected shots, such as only passing shots, kill shots, ceiling shots, etc."

Student Success Goal

- More than 60 percent of shots outside the detour zone

To Decrease Difficulty

- Decrease the Success Goal.
- Increase size of border.
- Decrease length of game.

To Increase Difficulty

- Increase the Success Goal.
- Decrease size of border.
- Increase length of game.

Shot Chart

Date _____

Player _____   Observer _____

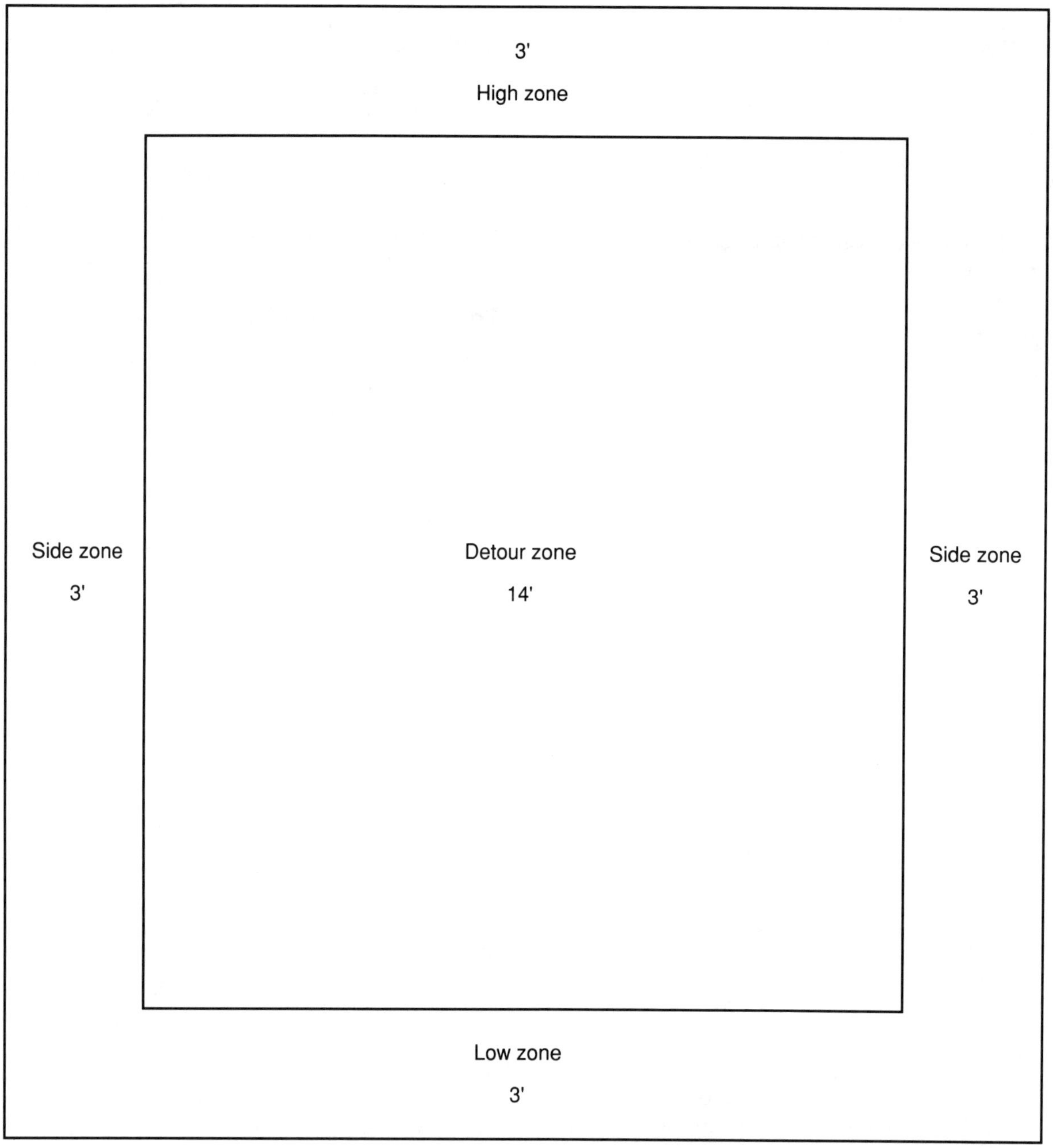

3'

High zone

Side zone

3'

Detour zone

14'

Side zone

3'

Low zone

3'

	Shots	Percentage
Low zone	_____	_____
Side zone	_____	_____
High zone	_____	_____
Detour zone	_____	_____
Total shots	_____	_____

Directions to observer: Watch only one player. Put an X on this chart (representing the front wall and the detour zone) where every shot hits. Include serves. If the wall is not marked, try to be as accurate as possible. Figure the percentage of each type of shot by dividing by the total number of shots taken. The percentages should total 100%.

Step 14   Cutthroat—For Fun and Improvement

Now is a good time to introduce cutthroat to your students. Some are tired of playing against the same people and always getting beaten. Some have improved rapidly and yearn for a higher level of competition. Others are frustrated by their lack of progress and especially their inability to return serves. Cutthroat and the cutthroat move-up tournament will satisfy students in all these categories.

INTRODUCING CUTTHROAT

A 5-minute introduction is usually sufficient for students to understand the difference between cutthroat and singles. Cutthroat is an unofficial game for three players. Each player keeps his or her own score. Server must announce all three scores prior to the serve. Example: Server would say, "2-5-0, first serve." When server loses rally, players rotate clockwise so a new doubles team is introduced against the new server.

When playing as a doubles team against the server, apply these doubles rules:

- Either player may play the ball when it is time for his or her team to return.
- A hinder cannot be called on one's partner.
- A ball returned toward the front wall and striking one's partner is loss of the rally.
- If one partner swings and misses, the other may legally return the ball if it is still in play.

RECEIVING STRATEGIES

It is helpful to demonstrate the two different formations for the doubles team. Have three players assume the positions and then explain the rationale and procedure for each formation. Lengthy explanations are not necessary; just cover the basic strong and weak points. Reminders while observing games will reinforce these points.

Side-by-Side Formation

The side-by-side formation (see Figure 14.1) is used for receiving serves and when on the defensive. It can be used all the time during play.

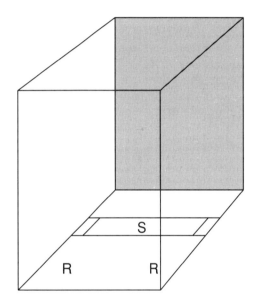

Figure 14.1   Side-by-side formation.

Strengths

- You start with this formation so you don't have to change. There is less chance for confusion.
- Both players can keep contact and communicate easily.
- It is hard for the server to use passing shots effectively.
- The stronger player can help the weaker player by covering more of the court.
- One player's backhand can be protected. That player should be on the forehand side of the stronger player. If one is right-handed and the other left-handed, the backhands should be to the midline.

Weaknesses

- This is not as strong defensively against kill shots.
- Players must move up and back together or else a weakness will be created.
- Players must communicate closely.
- Shots that go between the players might lead to confusion. The player with the forehand shot should always make the return.

Up-and-Back Formation

The up-and-back formation (Figure 14.2) is not good for receiving serves. Use it when you drive the singles player from center court. The front player assumes a position slightly in front of normal center court position and returns any shot he or she wishes, including volleys. The back player must be ready to return all shots, including those that get past front player.

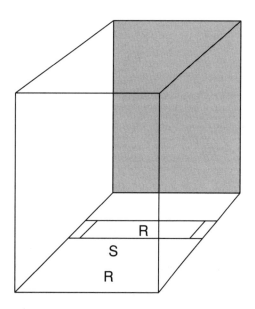

Figure 14.2   Up-and-back formation.

Strengths

- Can be helpful to kill weak returns by the singles player.
- Eliminates doubt and confusion about which player returns the shot.
- Can maneuver singles player from front to back.

- Can put players in position they like to play. Aggressive players make good "up" players. Less aggressive players get more time to think and react while playing the deep position.

Weaknesses

- The singles player can isolate the weaker player and work on him or her more easily.
- Down-the-line kills and passes can be effective against this formation.
- Front player cannot see back player and sometimes has difficulty deciding when to let shots go by. Communication is more difficult.
- Hard shots right at front player are hard to handle.

SERVING STRATEGIES

All players seem to like cutthroat. One appeal is that it eliminates the server's natural advantage, meaning fewer aces and more emphasis on strategy, shot selection, and shot quality. Advanced players look at this challenge as a way to improve the offensive part of their game. It does require more thinking and recognition of the doubles team's strengths and weaknesses. What follow are some shots and strategies you can mention to your students as you observe them playing cutthroat.

Against the Side-By-Side Formation

- Use kill shots if you are in front of them;
- do not pass, especially down-the-line;
- if you must pass, use a high (3 to 4 feet), softer cross-court pass;
- around-the-wall and Z-shots may work well if players don't communicate well (Step 17);
- sometimes surprise opponents by hitting shots down the center of the court, especially those that hit the side wall first and cross over the midline;
- try to work on the weaker player; and
- move the team up and back with ceiling shots or if one does not move up quickly, try a corner kill to that side. (Inside corner kill is best.)

Against the Up-and-Back Formation

- Down-the-line passing shots are best;
- do not kill if the front player is in front of you;
- hit the ball hard so the front player has less time to react;
- sometimes a ball right at the front player's feet is effective;

- ceiling shots to the backhand corner of the deep player are always a good option and might be followed with a down-the-line kill; and
- work on the weaker player.

Cutthroat Drill and Tournaments

1. *Cutthroat Drill*

[Corresponds to *Racquetball*, Step 14, Cutthroat Drill]

Group Management and Safety Tips

- Three players play per court.
- Extra player can chart shots in the detour zone for one of the other players.

Equipment

- Pencils
- Detour zone charts

Instructions to Class

There are three options when there are four players per court:

Option 1

- "Play cutthroat in your court. One player will have to wait outside while the three others play, but all four players will rotate in this game. Play the game as normal until the server loses serve. At that point the server becomes the waiter and a member of the doubles team becomes the server. The waiter comes into the court as a member of the new doubles team. Play continues for _____. [Determine the time period your students will play.]"

Option 2

- "Play a game of cutthroat in your court. One of the four players will have to sit out a game. The waiter should chart shots in the detour zone for one of the players. When one of the players scores _____ points, that player is the winner. [Determine the number of points a player needs to win.] Then everyone rotates. Take turns sitting out one game."

Option 3

- "Play a game of cutthroat in your court. One of the four players will have to sit out a game. The waiter should chart shots in the detour zone for one of the players. When one of the players scores _____ points, that player is the winner. [Determine the number of points a player needs to win.] The winner replaces the waiter and rests for one game. The two other players are joined by the person who was waiting. The object of this option is to have winners sit out and weaker players get more playing time."

Student Options

- "Decide for yourselves how to fairly rotate players into your court."
- "Modify the game so that only a certain type of shot, a kill shot for example, can win points."

Student Success Goals

- Win the most points under Option 1.
- Win half the games played under Option 2.
- Play no more than two games in a row under Option 3.

To Decrease Difficulty

- Use Option 1 and shorten the time period.
- Reduce the number of points it takes to win a game under Options 2 and 3.

To Increase Difficulty

- Use Option 1 and play for a longer time period.
- Use Options 2 or 3 and increase the number of points it takes to win a game.

2. *Move-Around Tournament*
[New Drill]

Court 1	Court 2	Court 3	Court 4	Court 5
1 →	1 →	1 →	1 →	1
2 ←	2 ←	2 ←	2 ←	2
3 →	3 →	3 →	3 →	3
4 ←	4 ←	4 ←	4 ←	4

Group Management and Safety Tips

- This tournament will allow players to play against people other than their usual opponents.
- Clearly post the number of each court.
- Post a rotation list outside each court so players know where to move next.

Instructions to Class

Assign each player in a court a number between 1 and 4. Play a game of cutthroat using the instructions under Option 1 in Drill 1. After time is called, players will rotate as follows:

For Middle Courts

- "Player 1 moves to the next higher court and remains player 1."
- "Player 2 goes to the next lower court and remains player 2."
- "Player 3 moves to next higher court and remains player 3."
- "Player 4 moves to the next lower court and remains player 4."

For the Lowest Court

- "Player 1 moves to the next higher court and remains player 1."
- "Player 2 becomes player 3."
- "Player 3 moves to the next higher court and remains player 3."
- "Player 4 becomes player 1."

For the Highest Court

- "Player 1 becomes player 4."
- "Player 2 moves to the next lower court and remains player 2."
- "Player 3 becomes player 2."
- "Player 4 moves to the next lower court and remains player 4."

3. *Winner Moves Up Tournament*
[New Drill]

Group Management and Safety Tips

- Use this tournament to assign new home courts that match players by ability.
- Clearly post the number of each court.
- Post rotation list outside each court so players are not confused.
- Allow for enough rounds so players finish in the highest court they can achieve.

Instructions to Class

- "In your home courts, play a game of cutthroat using the instructions under Option 1 (especially if time is a problem) or Option 3 in Drill 1. After time is called, players will rotate as follows."

In the Middle Courts

- "The winner will move up one court and the person with the lowest point total will move down one court for the next game. The person who was waiting will play the next game with the two new players while the player who finished second waits for the next game. The second-place player could play the next game if both new players are not there yet."

In the Top Court

- "The person with the lowest point total will move down one court, and the other three players will stay. The winner sits out the next game while the other three play."

In the Bottom Court

- "The player with the top score will move up, and the three others will stay. The person who finished second sits out the next game while the other three play. The second-place player could play the next game if the new player has not yet arrived."

Student Option

- "Use Option 1 in Drill 1. This could speed up the tournament."
- "Let someone else move up or down if they wish."

Student Success Goal

- Be at least one court higher at the end of the tournament

To Decrease Difficulty

- Play games to a lower point total.

To Increase Difficulty

- Play games to a higher point total.

Step 15 Z-Serves

At this stage in their development, some players will want to learn some new serves. The Z-serves, named after the path the ball travels (Figures 15.1 and 15.2), will give these players more variety to choose from to keep their opponents off balance. Some players will be having problems getting enough power on their hard serves and will like the soft Z-serve because they can master it and use it as a basic serve to supplement the lob serve.

The two Z-serves are different in many ways. Many beginners will not have the power or skill to execute the hard Z-serve, but practically all beginners will have some success with the soft Z-serve. The soft Z-serve is executed with the same soft touch and skill as the soft lob serves. Everyone will want to try both serves, but less-skilled players soon discover that the hard Z-serve is too difficult for them. At this point it is better to allow them to concentrate on the soft Z-serve. They will remember the hard Z-serve and come back to it when they have developed more skill and power.

Even powerful hitters will like the soft Z-serve because it is another off-speed serve they can use to change the pace of the game when playing an impatient or aggressive power player.

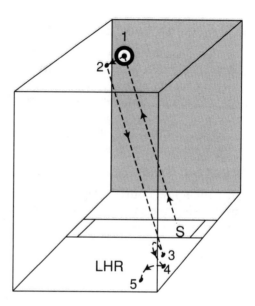

Figure 15.2 Ball path for the soft Z-serve to a left-handed receiver.

RETURNING Z-SERVES

Students usually have trouble returning both hard and soft Z-serves. You will have to remind them often to be patient and to get good position. Many will have trouble positioning themselves fast enough, so tell them to move quickly to the general area and make any final adjustments just before hitting the return.

Returning Hard Z-Serves

Review the basic receiving position with your students. They will have trouble returning serves unless they are on the midline and 6-8 feet from the back wall. From this position players can move quickly to a point facing the spot where the ball will come off the side wall and on the far side of the midline. They must decide how far the ball will rebound, but remind them that it is better to be too far away than too close. Students will soon discover they can move forward faster than backward.

Returning Soft Z-Serves

You must tell students the rules about returning the soft Z-serve. The serve may not be returned

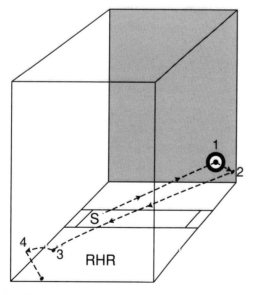

Figure 15.1 Ball path for hard Z-serve to a right-handed receiver.

until it has crossed the receiving line or has bounced in the safety zone (the area between the short line and the receiving line). This means students must judge how hard the serve is hit when deciding to attempt a return before the served ball bounces (a fly return) or after the first bounce. If the serve is going to bounce in the safety zone, students should retreat toward the rear corner and return the ball after it has bounced high and is dropping for a second bounce. The decision is even more difficult if the court has no receiving-line markings, and students must sometimes rely on their judgment.

If the serve will cross the receiving line before bouncing, a passing shot hit on the fly is an effective return. If possible, students can run around their backhand to hit a better return with their forehand. A ceiling shot from the corner is a good choice when students do not use the fly return.

As you introduce the hard and soft Z-serves, remind students of some of the important points of their proper execution as summarized in Figure 15.3.

Hard Z-Serve (Right- or left-handed server)	**Soft Z-Serve** (Right- or left-handed server)
For right-handed receivers:	**For right-handed receivers:**
Serve from near left side wall. **Target**—right corner about 3-4 feet high. **First bounce**—15-18 feet behind short serve line and 2-3 feet from the left side wall. **Second bounce**—15-18 feet behind short line and 3-8 feet from left side wall. **Receiver position**—normal. **Receiver moves to**—face left side wall and opposite where ball will hit the wall. Stay back from the side wall on opposite side of midline. Passing or ceiling shot return.	Serve from near left side wall. **Target**—right corner 3-4 feet below ceiling and 2 feet from side wall. **First bounce**—5 feet behind short serve line and 4-5 feet from opposite (left) side wall. **Second bounce**—Very near left rear corner. **Receiver position**—normal. **Receiver moves to**—First choice: Cut off serve on fly as it crosses the court (near midline). Pinch kill or passing shot. Second choice: Hit return soon after first bounce. Ceiling shot return.
For left-handed receivers:	**For left-handed receivers:**
Serve from near right side wall. **Target**—left corner about 3-4 feet high. **First bounce**: 15-18 feet behind short serve line and 2-3 feet from right side wall. **Second bounce**: 15-18 feet behind short serve line and 3-8 feet from right side wall. **Receiver position**—normal. **Receiver moves to**—face right side wall and opposite where ball will hit the wall. Stay back from side wall on opposite side of midline. Passing or ceiling shot return.	Serve from near right side wall. **Target**—left corner 3-4 feet below ceiling and 2 feet from side wall. **First bounce**: 5 feet behind short serve line and 4-5 feet from opposite (right) side wall. **Second bounce**: Very near right rear corner. **Receiver position**—normal. **Receiver moves to**—First choice: Cut off serve on fly as it crosses the court (near midline). Pinch kill or passing shot. Second choice: Hit return soon after first bounce. Ceiling shot return.

Figure 15.3 Z-serve summary chart.

STUDENT KEYS TO SUCCESS

Hard Z-Serves

- Move at an angle toward the target corner.
- Swing more underhand than sidearm.
- Keep backswing lower, almost behind body.
- Use a powerful swing.
- Hit to the receiver's backhand.
- Move quickly to center court.

Soft Z-Serves

- Face target corner squarely.
- Bounce ball high and out in front.
- Step toward corner.
- Use a good follow-through with racquet to add touch and control.
- Don't watch ball after the serve.
- Set up quickly at center court.

Z-Serve Rating

CHECKPOINT	BEGINNING LEVEL	INTERMEDIATE LEVEL	ADVANCED LEVEL
Hard Z-Serves Preparation	• Not applicable	• Nonracquet shoulder points to opposite corner • Backswing is normal for a forehand stroke	• Nonracquet shoulder points to opposite corner • Backswing is lower and almost behind body
Execution		• Ball is dropped toward opposite corner • Arm swing is mostly sidearm • Elbow and wrist do not rotate inward toward body and corner • Direction of movement is more toward front wall	• Ball is dropped toward opposite corner • Arm swing is mostly underhand • Elbow and wrist rotate inward toward body and corner • Direction of movement is toward opposite corner
Follow-Through		• Movement is rushed and jerky • Usually off balance • Racquet finishes low and to side of player	• Movement is smooth • Balance is good • Racquet finishes high and out in front of body
Soft Z-Serves Preparation	• Shoulders not always facing corner • Ball bounce is inconsistent (too low or too high, too close or too far away) • Weight often on front foot	• Usually facing corner • Ball bounce is usually accurate (moves into position to correct minor problems) • Weight usually on rear foot	• Good shoulder position • Ball bounce is accurate (correct height and distance from body) • Weight on rear foot

Z-Serve Rating

CHECKPOINT	BEGINNING LEVEL	INTERMEDIATE LEVEL	ADVANCED LEVEL
Execution	• Swing usually rushed and too hard • Amount of power very inconsistent (usually not enough) • Face of racquet often closed or open too much • Often hits ceiling or side wall first	• Makes good contact • Usually correct amount of power (sometimes too hard and ball comes too far away from walls) • Racquet face usually square to corner • Sometimes hits short serves and sometimes hits three-wall serve	• Smooth swing • Good touch and ball dies in corner • Racquet face at consistent angle toward corner • Seldom hits long or short • Ball hits walls at proper height, in correct sequence and at good angles
Follow-Through	• Swing usually stops at contact • Watches ball and does not move quickly to center court	• Inconsistent follow-through: too little or too much • Does not watch ball but is slow to move to center court	• Has compact follow-through • Does not watch ball after shot: recovers quickly and moves to center court

Error Detection and Correction for Z-Serves

The hard Z-Serve is difficult to execute successfully. Your students will know they lack the necessary power, but may not know why. If the problems are strength and hand-eye coordination, not much can be done except practice and training. If they wish, allow them to stop practicing the hard Z-serve because it will take a long time for them to develop enough skill and power. In the meantime, they can master other serves and enjoy playing until they develop sufficient power. Those with enough strength can benefit from your observations.

The most common problems you will see here are students having trouble changing the swing from sidearm to vertical and the inability to move diagonally toward the opposite corner. The drills in this step should help them solve these problems.

The problems with the soft Z-serve are fewer and less severe. If students can hit a good lob serve overhand, they will have good success with the soft Z-serve.

ERROR   **CORRECTION**

Hard Z-Serves

1. Swing is sidearm and parallel to the floor.

2. Serve does not contact second side wall deep enough.

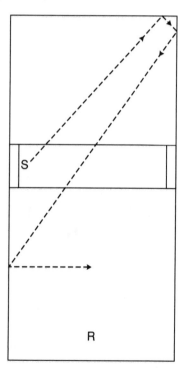

3. Server fails to shift weight toward corner during swing, resulting in lack of power.

1. Remind student of the need for a more underhanded swing. Have student go through slow-motion swing, while watching racquet head. (See Drill 1.)

2. This happens when the ball hits the front wall too close to the corner. Walk to the front wall and place your hand 2 feet from the corner and about 4 feet high. Have the server visualize hitting the spot before each serve. (See Drill 3.)

3. Remind server to move with serve. Place tape on floor and have server try to cross the tape while serving. (See Drill 3.)

ERROR 　　　　　　　　　　　　　　　　　**CORRECTION**

4. Server lunges at the ball trying to get enough power.

4. Have student start backswing slowly. Control comes when starting the motion slowly and deliberately, then building momentum and speed during the swing. Have student review the swing in slow motion.

5. Server "pulls head out" and fails to watch the ball.

5. This usually occurs when student tries to swing with power. Put two Xs on the ball with chalk (one opposite from the other) and ask student to try to see an X while serving the ball.

Soft Z-Serves

6. Student does not follow through, resulting in a serve that is too short or too soft.

6. Emphasize a complete swing, with less power. Have your student add power until the serve is too hard and long, then reduce the power slightly.

7. The serve does not cross over into the receiver's backhand corner.

7. The serve is not hitting close enough to the target corner. Have student try to hit as close to the corner as possible and observe the path of the serve.

8. Student has loss of accuracy because of not facing the corner squarely.

8. Place two strips of tape pointing to the target corner. Student should stay between the strips when serving.

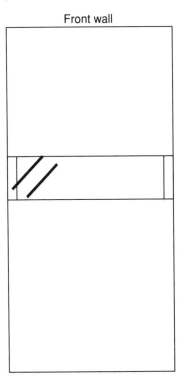

Front wall

ERROR 🚫   **CORRECTION**

9. Student does not shift weight from rear foot to front foot, resulting in lack of touch and control.

9. Start as in #8 and place a third strip of tape where rear foot should land while shifting weight forward.

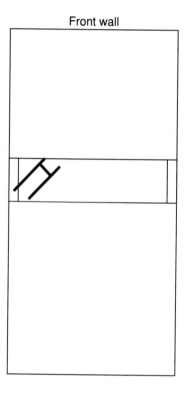

Front wall

10. The student does not move quickly to center court after executing the serve.

10. Remind student not to watch the serve but to concentrate on moving across in front of the serve. Have an observer yell "center court" right after the server contacts the ball.

Z-Serve Drills

1. Dry Run—Hard Z-Serves
[Corresponds to *Racquetball*, Step 15, Drill 1]

Group Management and Safety Tips

- Three or four players play on a court.
- All can learn by watching and visualizing.
- You could have all your students practice this movement in a large room or area so you could watch them all at once. If so, modify the instructions.
- Remove tape after drill.

Equipment

- Tape for marking floor (if in racquetball courts)

Instructions to Class

- "Start your Z-serve from this tape mark on the floor. Move toward the opposite corner while going through the serving motion. Remember to use more of an underhand swing and rotate your wrist and elbow in and forward while swinging. While wait-ing your turn, offer suggestions for improvement to the server. Also practice visualizing yourself as you would execute this serve."

Student Option

- "Practice the motions at a slower or faster pace."

Student Success Goal

- 10 dry-run hard Z-serves

To Decrease Difficulty

- Decrease the Success Goal.
- Ask server to go through serve in slow motion.

To Increase Difficulty

- Increase the Success Goal.
- Ask server to increase pace.

2. Dry Run—Soft Z-Serves
[Corresponds to *Racquetball*, Step 15, Drill 2]

Group Management and Safety Tips

- If you do this as a large group in a gymnasium or large room, modify the instructions.
- Three or four players play on a court.
- All can learn by watching and visualizing.
- With strips of tape, mark off a zone within the service area that points toward the corner to which the students will hit.
- Remove all markings from courts after class.

Equipment

- Tape to mark floor before class (if in racquetball courts)

Instructions to Class

- "Without a ball, practice your soft-Z-serve motion. Start from within these marks and step toward the opposite corner. Remember to face the corner squarely. Visualize bouncing a ball and contacting it high and then follow through. Pick a partner and have your partner observe you and offer suggestions."

Student Option

- "Practice anywhere."

Student Success Goal

- 10 dry-run soft Z-serves

To Decrease Difficulty

- Decrease the Success Goal.
- Ask server to go through serve in slow motion.

To Increase Difficulty

- Increase the Success Goal.
- Ask server to increase pace.

3. Hard Z-Serve

[Corresponds to *Racquetball*, Step 15, Drill 3]

Group Management and Safety Tips

- Three or four players play on a court.
- Observers can give tips for improvement.
- Before class, mark off a zone within the service area that points toward the corner to which the students will hit.
- Before class, mark target area on front wall near corner.
- Remove all marks from courts after class.

Equipment

- Tape for marking floor
- Two 2-foot by 2-foot cardboard boxes per court for targets (to increase difficulty)

Instructions to Class

- "Execute your hard Z-serve starting within these marks and moving toward the corner. Aim for the mark on the front wall 4 feet high and 2 feet from the corner. You and your courtmates observe where the ball strikes and what action is produced."

Student Options

- "Serve to the opposite wall. You may play a left-hander some day."
- "Set personal goals: five consecutive legal serves, etc."
- "Vary starting position and angle of approach."

Student Success Goal

- 10 legal hard Z-serves

To Decrease Difficulty

- Decrease the Success Goal.
- Serve into your backhand corner and "Z" off your forehand side wall.

To Increase Difficulty

- Increase the Success Goal.
- Count only serves that "Z" off wall within 5 feet of back wall.
- Add a box or similar target for serve to land in.

4. Soft Z-Serve With Partner

[Corresponds to *Racquetball*, Step 15, Drill 4]

Group Management and Safety Tips

- Before class, mark off a zone within the service area that points toward the corner to which the students will hit.
- Two to four players play per court.
- Extra students can observe drill, retrieve balls, and offer advice.
- Rotate turns.
- Remove marks from courts after class.

Equipment

- Tape to mark floor
- Two 2-foot by 2-foot cardboard boxes for targets for each court (to increase difficulty)

Instructions to Class

- "Start from within these marks and serve a soft Z-serve. Try to hit the front wall 2 feet from the corner and about 3 or 4 feet below the ceiling. Hit the serve softly, but remember to follow through. Try to make the ball die in the back corner after bouncing 2 to 4 feet behind the short line. Don't worry about moving to center court. Watch the bounces and learn how hard to hit the ball. Move your starting position if you want to change the angle a little bit."

Student Options

- "Vary the power to learn the right 'touch.' "
- "Serve to the other corner."

Student Success Goal

- 10 soft Z-serves

To Decrease Difficulty

- Decrease the Success Goal.

To Increase Difficulty

- Increase the Success Goal.
- Put a box or other target in the back corner to hit.

5. *Hard Z-Serves With Receiver Catch*

[Corresponds to *Racquetball*, Step 15, Drill 5]

Group Management and Safety Tips

- Four players play on a court.
- Students not serving or receiving can retrieve balls, offer observations, and rotate in for their turn.

Equipment

- 1 basket or ball glove per court (to decrease difficulty)

Instructions to Class

- "Server executes a hard Z-serve, then moves to center court to set up. Observer notes server's movement and whether server looks back. Receiver judges speed and angle of serve and moves to proper position from receiving position. Receiver has no racquet but attempts to catch ball while it is still in play. The second observer will note the receiver's position and movement and offer suggestions."

- "Observers should stand near forehand side wall."

Student Options

- "Server and receiver can make a contest out of drill."
- "Observers can give audio cues to server and receiver to move."

Student Success Goal

- 7 out of 10 catches of legal hard Z-serves

To Decrease Difficulty

- Decrease the Success Goal.
- Allow receiver to use basket or ball glove to catch ball.

To Increase Difficulty

- Increase the Success Goal.

6. *Soft Z-Serves With Receiver Catch*

[Corresponds to *Racquetball*, Step 15, Drill 6]

Group Management and Safety Tips

- Four players play per court.
- Extra students can observe, offer suggestions, or retrieve balls.
- Rotate turns.
- Remove all marks from courts after class.

Equipment

- Tape to mark receiver's starting position (to increase difficulty)

Instructions to Class

- "The server serves a soft Z-serve. The receiver, who has no racquet, tries to catch the ball after it crosses the receiving line or immediately after it hits the floor. The receiver should start from a normal receiving position each time. Attempt to catch the first 10 serves in this way. Then let the next 10 bounce to the back corner. Attempt to catch them between the first and second bounces. Receivers give feedback about the quality of the serve and the best place to try to return it."

Student Options

- "Decide how to play each serve individually."
- "Make a contest between server and receiver."

Student Success Goals

- Catch 7 out of 10 serves before the first bounce or immediately after the ball bounces in the safety zone.
- Catch 7 out of 10 serves between the first and second bounces.

To Decrease Difficulty

- Decrease Success Goals.

To Increase Difficulty

- Increase Success Goals.
- Mark receiver's position on floor with tape. Receiver must stay in position until serve is struck.

7. *Return of Hard Z-Serve by Receiver With Observer*
[Corresponds to *Racquetball*, Step 15, Drill 7]

Group Management and Safety Tips

- Two players play per court.
- An observer can watch and keep score from outside the court.
- Players and observers rotate tasks.

Instructions to Class

- "The server serves a hard Z-serve. The receiver tries to return it with a ceiling shot or a passing shot. The server moves quickly to set up at center court. The server then tries to trap the ball between his or her racquet and hand. Observer scores the number of successful returns by receiver and also movement of server."

Student Options

- "Server and receiver can make a contest out of the drill: 1 point for the return by receiver, 1 point for a catch of the return by the server."
- "Vary the angle and placement of serve."
- "Serve to the forehand of the receiver."

Student Success Goal

- 7 out of 10 returns of service by receiver

To Decrease Difficulty

- Decrease the Success Goal.

To Increase Difficulty

- Increase the Success Goal.
- Require a specific shot for the return.

8. *Return of Soft Z-Serve by Receiver With Observer*
[Corresponds to *Racquetball*, Step 15, Drill 8]

Group Management and Safety Tips

- Two players play per court.
- Observers can watch and keep score from outside the court.
- Players and observers rotate tasks.

Instructions to Class

- "The server serves 10 soft Z-serves. The receiver tries to return them before the first bounce. Remember, the receiver may not play the serve in front of the receiving line until it has bounced. To return the serve on the fly in front of the line is a violation and would be a point for the server. If the serve bounces in front of the receiving line, do not try to return it and do not count it as a trial for the server. Have the server serve another in its place. The return should be either a pinch kill or a passing shot. The server moves to the ready position right after the serve and attempts to trap the return between his or her racquet and hand. The receiver attempts to return the next 10 serves between the first and second bounce.

These returns should be ceiling shots. The server also attempts to trap these returns. Observers keep count and also observe quality of movement by server and returns by receiver."

Student Options

- "Decide how to return each serve individually."
- "Make a contest between the server and receiver."

Student Success Goals

- 7 out of 10 successful returns before the first bounce
- 7 out of 10 successful returns between the first and second bounces

To Decrease Difficulty

- Decrease Success Goals.

To Increase Difficulty

- Increase Success Goals.
- Require a specific return shot.

9. *Z-Serve Game*
[Corresponds to *Racquetball*, Step 15, Drill 9]

Group Management and Safety Tips

- This is an excellent game for both server and receiver.
- Two players play per court.
- Other players can observe, chart server or receiver, or practice other drills while waiting their turn.

Equipment

- Paper and pencils

Instructions to Class

- "Play a game to 7 points with an opponent. Alternate turns at service regardless of who wins the point. Use only soft Z-serves. The server gets 1 point if the receiver fails to make a legal return. The receiver gets 1 point for a legal return of service. Servers do not play the return. The receiver may not play the serve in front of the receiving line until it has bounced. Play three games. Rotate with the waiters and let them play three games. Then, using the same rules, repeat the entire drill using the hard Z-serve."

Student Options

- "Play the game using only soft Z-serves."
- "Change the number of points for receiver returns. For example: 2 for fly returns, 1 for others."
- "Server can mix hard and soft Z-serves."

Student Success Goals

- Win two out of three soft Z-serve games
- Win two out of three hard Z-serve games

To Decrease Difficulty

- Play games to fewer than 7 points.
- Play fewer games.

To Increase Difficulty

- Play games to more than 7 points.
- Play more games.

10. *Z-Serve Tournament*
[New Drill]

Group Management and Safety Tips

- Use this tournament to determine best players within each court.
- Can use a move-up format as in the cutthroat move-up tournament.
- You could limit games to soft Z-serves, hard Z-serves, or give servers their choices.

Instructions to Class

- "Play games to 7 points within your court. Use only a soft Z-serve or a hard Z-serve. Play everyone in your court."

Success Goal

- Assuming four players to a court, win two of three games; otherwise, win half or more of games played

To Decrease Difficulty

- Decrease the Success Goal.
- Play games to fewer than 7 points.

To Increase Difficulty

- Increase the Success Goal.
- Play games to more than 7 points.

Step 16   Strategy Rule #5— High-High, Low-Low

Relate this strategy rule to the detour zone strategy rule when you introduce it to your students. It will help them further improve their shot quality and help them decide which shots to use. Tell students that this rule has three specific meanings. The first two are fairly obvious: If a ball comes to you high, return it high. If a ball comes to you low, return it low. Students usually relate well to these two parts of "High-High, Low-Low." It helps them decide easily which type of shot to choose. However, it is important to go over carefully with your students the second meaning of "Low-Low": If they wish to hit a low shot off a high ball they have to be patient enough to let the ball drop low. You might even give them examples of when this might happen. The classic example is when an opponent's ceiling shot does not have the proper angle for the ball to go deep near the back wall. Then the returner has the choice of playing the ball high or waiting for it to drop low.

Waiting for the ball to drop low requires confidence in one's skills. Not everyone has that confidence. To help students who do not grasp the physics involved, explain that the rebound angle is the same as the approach angle. Thus, if a ball is hit downward from waist or shoulder height and contacts the front wall low, it will rebound at an equal angle—waist or shoulder high—and be easy for the opponent to handle. Be patient and explain repeatedly why a player must wait for the ball to drop low before attempting a kill shot or a low passing shot. It is worth spending some time explaining, because you cannot assume students are progressing in their use of strategy just because they are quickly improving physically.

STUDENT KEYS TO SUCCESS

- Get into position early.
- Make decision early whether high or low.
- If bounce is high, hit high return.
- If low, move with ball, waiting for it to drop.
- If waiting for high bounce to drop, use time to determine position of opponent and plan shot.

Rating for Strategy Rule #5—High-High, Low-Low

CHECKPOINT	BEGINNING LEVEL	INTERMEDIATE LEVEL	ADVANCED LEVEL
Preparation	• Arrives late • Not aware of opponent	• Arrives in time • Notices opponent	• Arrives early • Plans shot to take advantage of opponent's position
Execution	• Returns high ball at first opportunity	• Returns high ball before necessary	• Waits to return high ball with low shot when appropriate
Follow-Through	• Stands and watches return	• Usually moves to center court	• Moves quickly and easily to center court and anticipates return

Error Detection and Correction for Strategy Rule #5

The errors in this area are primarily mental. You need to reassure some of your students that they have time to wait on the ball and plan their shot. This comes naturally to some, but others need experience and coaching.

ERROR

CORRECTION

1. Player hits many shots at a level between knees and shoulders.

2. Player hits waist-high ball on downward angle trying for kill shot.

3. Player does not remember to hit ceiling shots when they are in order.

1. Ask player to make a choice to play the ball below the knees or above the shoulders. Have a courtmate chart this habit.

2. Demonstrate to student that all such shots rebound high and would be easy to return. Have student hit 10 shots like that. Then hit 10 shots using paper cups to hit from as in Step 12, Drill 1.

3. Have student play a game using normal rules with one exception: Award 2 extra points for a ceiling shot that ends the rally.

High-High, Low-Low Drills

1. Ceiling Shot—Kill Shot
[Corresponds to *Racquetball*, Step 16, Drill 1]

Group Management and Safety Tips
- Two players play per court.
- Other players should observe and give feedback when drill is over.

Instructions to Class
- "Start a ceiling shot rally with a partner. Wait for a ceiling shot that rebounds only to center court. Wait for the ball to drop and execute any type of kill shot. The other player tries to return the kill shot with a low return (usually another kill shot). If neither shot ends the rally, do not continue the rally. Stop and restart the drill with a ceiling shot."

Student Options
- "Play out the rally."
- "Award points for kill shots or returns."
- "Allow players to attempt kill shots if ceiling shots come off back wall a long way (into center court)."

Student Success Goal
- 5 repetitions of drill

To Decrease Difficulty
- Decrease the Success Goal.
- Have player intentionally hit poor ceiling shot.

To Increase Difficulty
- Increase the Success Goal.

2. *Game Situation—Seven-Point Games*
[Corresponds to *Racquetball*, Step 16, Drill 2]

Group Management and Safety Tips

- Two players play per court.
- Other players chart shots while waiting their turns.

Equipment

- Paper and pencils

Instructions to Class

- "Play a game to 7 points. Have an observer chart the number of balls that come to you at waist height or above. At this stage, you should return at least 80 percent of them with a high shot. Right now that means a ceiling shot, but in the next step you will learn more shots. Also have the observer record the number that come to you below your waist. You should return at least 80 percent of them with a low shot. This means low passing shots and kill shots. When the game is over exchange roles. Observers become players, and players become observers."

Student Options

- "Play cutthroat."
- "If no observers are available, give feedback to each other after each game."
- "Remind each other verbally during the game to return high or return low."

Student Success Goals

- 80 percent of high balls returned high
- 80 percent of low balls returned low

To Decrease Difficulty

- Decrease Success Goals.
- Play games to fewer than 7 points.

To Increase Difficulty

- Increase Success Goals.
- Play games to more than 7 points.

3. *Remember the Ceiling Shot*
[New Drill]

Group Management and Safety Tips

- Two players play per court.
- Could play cutthroat.
- Rotate players in after every three games.

Instructions to Class

- "This is a good drill to help you remember to use ceiling shots whenever the opportunity arises. Play a game to 7 points using normal rules with one exception: 2 bonus points are awarded to either server or receiver when they hit a ceiling shot that ends the rally. Play a total of three games."

Student Options

- "Award 1 bonus point for each ceiling shot, more for rally-ending ceiling shots."
- "Award bonus points for quality kill shots also."

Student Success Goal

- Win two of three games

To Decrease Difficulty

- Decrease the Success Goal.
- Play games to fewer than 7 points.
- Award 3 points for a ceiling shot that ends the rally.

To Increase Difficulty

- Increase the Success Goal.
- Play games to more than 7 points.
- Require ceiling shot to be to backhand corner.

Step 17 **Z-Shot and Around-the-Wall Shot**

Ask your students this question: "What do you do when you get pulled up in front of the service line by a long rebound off the back wall?" In answer, your students probably will suggest the dink, or soft kill, in the corner and the low hard passing shot. These are good options that you should discuss with your students. The dink or soft kill in the corner should be used when your opponent stays back around center court or deeper. The low hard passing shot should be kept near the side walls and should be used when your opponent is in front of the short line or coming forward late and fast.

But if you guess wrong about your opponent's strategy, you probably will lose the rally. Safer options are the Z-shot and around-the-wall shot. These shots will not win as many rallies, but neither will they lose as many. So if you are not sure of your opponent's strategy, or if you just want to buy time to get back to a safer position in center court, use the Z-shot or around-the-wall shot. In addition, they make the soft kill and the low hard passing shot more effective

because your opponent will have to cover more options.

Students may have a hard time visualizing the shots, so demonstrate them yourself or have an advanced student hit the shots while you point out the mechanics. Use the Z-shot when the ball is high and near the front court and to either side of the imaginary midline. The Z-shot is executed like the Z-serve except that it is hit high off the front wall near the corner opposite the player. It ricochets off the front wall to the adjacent wall, then to the opposite wall, and then dies in the back corner (Figure 17.1).

As you demonstrate the around-the-wall shot, emphasize that it should be hit only when the ball is high in the front court near the imaginary midline. The ball is hit high on a side wall, near the corner. It ricochets off the side wall to the front wall, bounces to the other side wall, then crosses the court downward, hits off the opposite side wall, and dies in the corner (Figure 17.2).

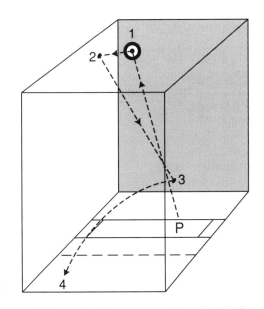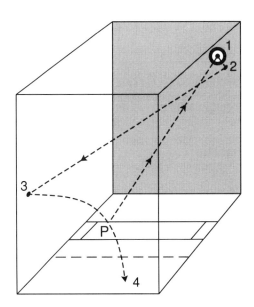

Figure 17.1   Z-shot to left front corner (a) and right front corner (b).

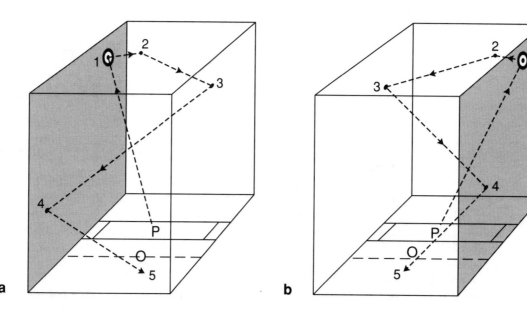

Figure 17.2   Around-the-wall shot to left front corner (a) and right front corner (b).

STUDENT KEYS TO SUCCESS
Z-Shot

- Hit this shot when the ball is high and in front of the short line and on either side of the imaginary midline.
- Execute like a Z-serve only target is higher.
- Hit ball hard into opposite corner. Hit front wall first.
- Return quickly to center court.
- Anticipate lengthy wait for return.

Around-the-Wall Shot

- Hit this shot when the ball is high and in front of the short line and on the imaginary midline.
- Hit ball high and hard into corner. Hit side wall first.
- Return quickly to center court.
- Anticipate lengthy wait for return.

Z-Shot and Around-the-Wall Shot Rating

CHECKPOINT	BEGINNING LEVEL	INTERMEDIATE LEVEL	ADVANCED LEVEL
Preparation	• Does not anticipate long bounce off back wall • Usually cannot catch up with ball	• Sometimes underestimates length of bounce • Catches up with ball just in time to hit it	• Runs toward front wall as ball heads toward back wall • Gets good position early and has time to determine position of opponent

Z-Shot and Around-the-Wall Shot Rating

CHECKPOINT	BEGINNING LEVEL	INTERMEDIATE LEVEL	ADVANCED LEVEL
Execution	• Often off balance • Poor position to hit ball • Lunges at ball • Swing is jerky	• Inconsistent body control (sometimes disoriented) • Inconsistent position on ball • Swing is hurried	• Good body control • Good position • Eyes on ball • Strong, smooth stroke
Results	• Ball often hits ceiling or is too low when crossing court • Ball does not get deep to backcourt • Opponent often kills shot or hits effective passing shot	• Ball is not high enough crossing court • Opponent often cuts ball off at midcourt • Opponent's shot usually keeps player on defensive	• Ball stays high while crossing court • Opponent is driven deep to return ball • Opponent usually hits weak, defensive return

Error Detection and Correction for the Z-Shot and Around-the-Wall Shot

You may have to watch your students play a lot before you see an opportunity for one of these shots, which complicates your need to know whether they are using the shots when they can. You also can ask your students how often they hit these shots. Indeed, the most common error is to fail to use them. Observing your students in drills is the best way to make sure students are using correct techniques.

ERROR

CORRECTION

1. Student fails to use the shots when the opportunity is presented.

1. Stop the game immediately and discuss the situation. Try to determine why shots are not used. Encourage the student to use the game situation bonus point explained in Drill 5.

2. Student has trouble getting enough power on shot.

2. Have student use same footwork as for Z-serve. Move toward corner, transfer weight, and follow through on racquet swing.

ERROR 🚫	CORRECTION
3. Student selects wrong type of shot: Z-shot versus around-the wall shot.	3. When in doubt, use the Z-shot. It is much more effective. Use the around-the-wall shot only when you are on the midline. Even then, sometimes the Z-shot is better.
4. The ball hits the ceiling and does not have the action of either shot.	4. The student has contacted the ball too low. Either get to the ball sooner and hit the shot when the ball is high in the air or choose another shot. A passing shot or soft corner kill shot would be logical choices.

Z-Shot and Around-the-Wall Shot Drills

1. Z-Shot
[Corresponds to *Racquetball*, Step 17, Drill 1]

Group Management and Safety Tips
- Three to four players play on each court.
- Observer notes target area and action of the ball.
- Observer gives feedback.
- Others retrieve balls.
- Rotate turns.

Equipment
- 2 cardboard boxes (about 2 feet by 2 feet) per court for targets in back corners (to increase difficulty)

Instructions to Class
- "From a spot 4 to 6 feet away from your forehand wall, bounce the ball high as for a lob serve. Execute a Z-shot into the opposite corner with your forehand stroke. Hit five from the service line and five from the short line. From the service line, you want to hit the front wall about 4 to 6 feet from the corner and about 5 feet down from the ceiling. Have your partner watch the target and the shot and give you feedback. Change the target slightly if your shot does not get deep enough. This will vary with your angle and location, but if you are deeper in the court, you need to hit closer to the corner. After five forehand shots from each spot, take five backhand shots from each spot. Then rotate until each has had their turn."

Student Options
- "Try the shot from other locations on the court."
- "Contact the ball at different heights to observe action."
- "Set personal goals for accuracy and placement."

Student Success Goal
- 15 Z-shots with each stroke from each position

To Decrease Difficulty
- Decrease the Success Goal.
- Have someone else bounce the ball for the shot.

To Increase Difficulty
- Increase the Success Goal.
- Place targets (such as boxes) near back wall and corner to try to hit.
- Try to get 11 out of 15 to "Z" off the side wall within 5 feet of the back wall.

2. *Z-Shot With Partner Return*
[Corresponds to *Racquetball*, Step 17, Drill 2]

Group Management and Safety Tips

- Two players play per court.
- Observers can chart shots and make notes from outside the court.
- Exchange feedback and roles.

Equipment

- Paper and pencils

Instructions to Class

- "One person hits a Z-shot. The other, starting from center court, tries to make a good return using a ceiling shot or a passing shot. Remember the shot will bounce a long way after hitting the side wall. Sometimes it is best to let it bounce off the opposite side wall before returning it. The first player should quickly move to center court and face the front wall. Do not play the return. After 15 shots with each stroke, exchange places."

Student Options

- "The first player can try to catch the return."

- "Returner can grade the quality of the shot such as A, B, C, or D."
- "Make a contest between the first and second players: 1 point for a Z-shot that goes deep, 2 points for a return."

Student Success Goals

- Return 10 out of 15 Z-shots hit with forehand
- Return 10 out of 15 Z-shots hit with backhand

To Decrease Difficulty

- Decrease Success Goals.
- Returner can start from deep in the back court.

To Increase Difficulty

- Increase Success Goals.
- Returner starts from short line or higher.
- Limit returns to ceiling shots only or passing shots only.

3. *Around-the-Wall Shot*
[Corresponds to *Racquetball*, Step 17, Drill 3]

Group Management and Safety Tips

- Four players play per court.
- Observer notes target and action of ball.
- Observer gives feedback.
- Others retrieve balls.
- Rotate turns.
- Observers must wait in center court area and be alert so they do not get hit with the ball or interfere with bounces.

Equipment

- 2 cardboard boxes (about 2 feet by 2 feet) per court for targets in back corners (to increase difficulty)

Instructions to Class

- "From a spot near the midline, bounce the ball high as for a lob serve. Hit an around-the-wall shot into the corner, hitting the side wall first about 5 feet below the ceiling. The ball should hit 2 to 5 feet from the corner depending on how deep you are in the court. Hit five from the service line and five from the short serve line. Hit closer to the corner as you move back. Hit the ball high and hard and watch the bounces. Repeat the drill using your backhand into the other corner."

Student Options

- "Try the shot from other locations on the court."
- "Contact the ball at different heights to observe action."
- "Set personal goals for accuracy and placement."

Student Success Goal

- 15 around-the-wall shots with both fore-hand and backhand strokes

To Decrease Difficulty

- Decrease the Success Goal.
- Have someone else bounce the ball for the shot.

To Increase Difficulty

- Increase the Success Goal.
- Place targets (such as boxes) near back wall and corners to try to hit.
- Try to get 7 out of 10 shots to bounce for the second time within 5 feet of the back wall.

4. Around-the-Wall Shot With Partner Return
[Corresponds to *Racquetball*, Step 17, Drill 4]

Group Management and Safety Tips

- Two players play per court.
- Observers can chart shots and make notes from outside court.
- Exchange feedback and roles.

Equipment

- Paper and pencils

Instructions to Class

- "One person hits an around-the-wall shot. The other, starting from center court, tries to make a good return using a ceiling shot or a passing shot. Remember the ball will bounce high and hard. It may be better to let it bounce off more than one wall before you return it. The first player should return quickly to center court and set up facing the front wall. Do not play the return. After 10 shots with each stroke, exchange places."

Student Options

- "The first player can try to catch the return between racquet and hand."

- "Returner can grade the quality of the shot, such as A, B, C, or D."
- "Make a contest between the first and second player giving 1 point for a good shot and 2 points for a return."

Student Success Goal

- Return 10 out of 15 around-the-wall shots, with both forehand and backhand shots.

To Decrease Difficulty

- Decrease the Success Goal.
- Returner starts from deep in back court.

To Increase Difficulty

- Increase the Success Goal.
- Returner starts from short serve line or higher.
- Limit returns to only ceiling shots or passing shots.

5. Game Situation

[Corresponds to *Racquetball*, Step 17, Drill 5]

Group Management and Safety Tips

- Can play as single or cutthroat games.
- Extra players could take notes, chart shots, or keep score.
- Extra players rotate turns each game.

Equipment

- Paper and pencils

Instructions to Class

- "Play a game to 15 points. Play all regular rules except 2 bonus points are awarded whenever a player uses a Z-shot or around-the-wall shot. The points are added to the score as they occur. Either the server or receiver can score bonus points."

Student Options

- "Play to different scores."
- "Make up other special rules to encourage the use of these shots."

Student Success Goal

- Win two out of three games

To Decrease Difficulty

- Shorten games.

To Increase Difficulty

- Lengthen games.
- Require Z-shots and around-the-wall shots to be nonreturnable for bonus points to be awarded.

Step 18   Strategy Rule #6— Never Change a Winning Game, Always Change a Losing Game

This strategy rule ties together all other basic strategy rules. It is so simple and logical that you at first may be embarrassed to discuss it. But if you discuss this rule in detail with your students, you will discover they can relate to the rule but don't comprehend the depth of it, that they seldom use positive mental techniques to pull themselves out of a losing streak. By discussing the techniques in this step, you may be able to trigger those positive thoughts when they need them. It is difficult to tell what players are thinking while you watch them play, but if you systematically guide them through the following trouble areas, you can help them overcome bad habits through brain power. These trouble areas are more fully explained in the participant's book (Step 18).

RECEIVING POSITION

Many students start too deep in the court and shade toward their backhand side too much while getting ready to receive a serve. Demonstrate how to turn to touch the back wall with the racquet, then take two steps toward the front wall. Students will remember this easily and it will be the first step toward successfully returning serves. Students waiting to play can observe or record the receiver's position on each serve. Use tape to mark the receiving area (Step 7, Corrections 5 and 6).

RETURN OF SERVICE

You can easily check to see if students have a backhand grip while waiting for the serve. It is much harder to tell if they are watching the server's body movement or the ball. Probably the only way to determine this is to ask them. Ceiling shots and passing shots are the two best returns of service and are easily observable. Anything else is usually a low percentage shot. Students waiting their turn to play can chart returns of service for a player.

SERVING

It seems impossible to believe, but many beginners serve to their opponent's forehand without realizing it. Another common problem is that students neglect to use the lob serves enough, if at all. Use Drill 1 to chart every player at least once to demonstrate serving habits and accuracy. Students naturally will want to work on their power serve and will need help only with velocity and placement.

DURING PLAY

Players commit many errors during play. A discussion of recent games will help pinpoint the solution. Players often have a feel for these problems and need only encouragement and advice to solve them by themselves. Encouraging classmates to observe and offer suggestions can help.

The most common problem beginners have is failure to hit enough ceiling shots. Observation and/or charting of games will help this problem.

The second most common problem is overuse of power, especially on passing shots. Have classmates chart the number of setups one gives an opponent off the back wall. This will create an awareness of the problem, and solutions often follow awareness.

BACK WALL TO FRONT WALL RETURN

Hitting the ball into the back wall to return it to the front wall is a bad habit both common to beginners and easy to break. When you see this shot, remind students of its two disadvantages: 1) It usually results in a weak return to the front wall if the shot gets there at all. 2) Continuing to use this return means that your backhand will not improve as much as you need. Surprisingly, students don't usually figure this out themselves and will continue to use this shot if not corrected.

BE PATIENT

Patience and confidence go hand in hand, but it is hard to try to instill confidence in your students. Patience and confidence usually come with practice, success, and experience, and you can help your students develop these feelings. Many players panic when they get way behind or when their opponent gets within a few points of winning the game. Discuss this feeling with students and try to get them to set very short-term goals such as taking away the serve or winning the next point. Drills 3, 4, and 5 can help. When your students can set and achieve these short-term goals, they use patience and concentration to overcome panic.

REVIEW THE STRATEGY RULES

It may surprise you how differently students adopt these strategies. Some will use these strategies from the first day. Others will have trouble even remembering what they are. You can help this second group by review and repetition. Another segment will be able to recite the rules but can't use them during games. This third group needs to examine which shot patterns and strategies they are using. If they are having success, they must be doing something correctly. But they will most remember the games or situations in which they did not have success. And it is here that this technique will be effective. Go over each rule and ask questions about each strategy. You will be able to pinpoint part of their problems—even without watching them play.

Strategy Rule #6 Drills

1. *Chart Lob and Power Serves*
[New Drill]

Group Management and Safety Tips

- Two players play per court.
- Observers chart serves from outside court.
- Exchange roles after each game.
- Reproduce service chart before class.
- You can use results as part of student evaluation.

Equipment

- Service charts
- Pencils

Instructions to Class

- "Two players play a game to 7 points. Each player has an observer to chart the player's serves. Observers should circle the appropriate response according to the directions on the chart. If you need help interpreting any part of the chart be sure to ask."

Student Options

- "Play longer or shorter games."
- "Have observers chart other items."
- "One observer could chart both servers if necessary."

Student Success Goals

- 90 percent of serves to receiver's backhand
- 50 percent are quality serves

To Decrease Difficulty

- Decrease the Success Goals.
- Lower standards for quality serves.

To Increase Difficulty

- Increase the Success Goals.
- Raise standards for quality serves (such as unreturnable or aces).

Service chart

Date: _____

Player: _____   Observer: _____

Lob serve   ## Power serve

		To backhand		Quality serve					To backhand		Quality serve	
1	2	Yes	No	Yes	No		1	2	Yes	No	Yes	No
1	2	Yes	No	Yes	No		1	2	Yes	No	Yes	No
1	2	Yes	No	Yes	No		1	2	Yes	No	Yes	No
1	2	Yes	No	Yes	No		1	2	Yes	No	Yes	No
1	2	Yes	No	Yes	No		1	2	Yes	No	Yes	No
1	2	Yes	No	Yes	No		1	2	Yes	No	Yes	No
1	2	Yes	No	Yes	No		1	2	Yes	No	Yes	No
1	2	Yes	No	Yes	No		1	2	Yes	No	Yes	No
1	2	Yes	No	Yes	No		1	2	Yes	No	Yes	No
1	2	Yes	No	Yes	No		1	2	Yes	No	Yes	No
1	2	Yes	No	Yes	No		1	2	Yes	No	Yes	No
1	2	Yes	No	Yes	No		1	2	Yes	No	Yes	No
1	2	Yes	No	Yes	No		1	2	Yes	No	Yes	No
1	2	Yes	No	Yes	No		1	2	Yes	No	Yes	No
1	2	Yes	No	Yes	No		1	2	Yes	No	Yes	No
1	2	Yes	No	Yes	No		1	2	Yes	No	Yes	No
1	2	Yes	No	Yes	No		1	2	Yes	No	Yes	No
1	2	Yes	No	Yes	No		1	2	Yes	No	Yes	No
1	2	Yes	No	Yes	No		1	2	Yes	No	Yes	No
1	2	Yes	No	Yes	No		1	2	Yes	No	Yes	No
1	2	Yes	No	Yes	No		1	2	Yes	No	Yes	No
1	2	Yes	No	Yes	No		1	2	Yes	No	Yes	No
1	2	Yes	No	Yes	No		1	2	Yes	No	Yes	No

Totals ___ ___   ___ ___   ___ ___   Totals ___ ___   ___ ___   ___ ___

Quality lob serve
1. Does not hit side wall before it is near back wall.
2. Bounces twice before it gets to back wall.
3. If it hits the back wall before it bounces twice, it hits only 2 feet high.

Quality power serve
1. Must bounce twice before contacting side or back wall.
2. Ball hits 2 feet or lower on front wall.
3. Ball stays close to side wall.

Directions to observer: Circle the 1 if this serve was the first attempt at this point. Circle 2 if it was the second. Circle yes if the serve forced the receiver to use the backhand for the return, no if it didn't. Circle yes if the serve was a quality serve, no if it wasn't. The requirements for a quality serve are listed above. All the conditions must be met to be a quality serve.

2. *Return of Service Chart*
[New Drill]

Group Management and Safety Tips

- You'll need two players and one or two observers.
- Observer charts from outside court.
- Exchange data and roles after each game.
- This can be done at the same time as Drill 1.
- You can use results as part of student evaluation.

Equipment

- Return of service charts
- Pencils

Instructions to Class

- "Two players play a game to 7 points. The observer will tally returns of service by category and placement. Ceiling shots and passing shots would be best options. The returns should be to the server's backhand in most cases. Compare the percentage of desirable returns with the final score."

Student Option

- "Record other shots after return of service."

Student Success Goal

- Return 75 percent of services with a ceiling shot or passing shot to the server's backhand.

To Decrease Difficulty

- Decrease the Success Goal.

To Increase Difficulty

- Increase the Success Goal.
- Require only ceiling shots or only passing shots.

Return of service chart

Serve	Ceiling shot	Passing shot	Other	Comments
1				
2				
3				
4				
5				
6				
7				
8				
9				
10				
11				
12				
13				
14				
15				
16				
17				
18				
19				
20				
21				
22				
23				
24				
25				
26				
27				
28				
29				
30				
31				
32				

3. *One-Point Game*

[Corresponds to *Racquetball*, Step 18, Drill 1]

Group Management and Safety Tips

- Two players play on a court.
- Others can chart serves or other shots while waiting their turns.

Equipment

- Charts
- Pencils

Instructions to Class

- "Play a game to 1 point against an opponent. This will help you concentrate and focus on 1 point at a time. Play eight games against the same opponent, alternating turns at service. Play each courtmate if time permits."

Student Options

- "Arrange 1-point game tournaments within your court."
- "Same player starts serving every game."

Student Success Goal

- Win five or more games against each opponent

To Decrease Difficulty

- Decrease the Success Goal.
- Play lesser-skilled players.
- Same player starts serving every game.

To Increase Difficulty

- Increase the Success Goal.
- Play higher-skilled players.
- Same player starts receiving every game.

4. *Two-Point Game*

[Corresponds to *Racquetball*, Step 18, Drill 2]

Group Management and Safety Tips

- Two players play per court.
- Others can chart serves or other shots while waiting their turns.

Equipment

- Charts
- Pencils

Instructions to Class

- "Play a game to 7 points against an opponent. The server gets 1 point for winning the rally. The receiver gets 2 points for winning the rally. Alternate serves. This game will help you concentrate on taking the serve away from your opponent. Play as many games as time allows."

Student Option

- "Change point allowances for server and receiver."

Student Success Goal

- Win 50 percent or more of games played

To Decrease Difficulty

- Decrease the Success Goal.
- Play shorter games.
- Play lesser-skilled players.

To Increase Difficulty

- Increase the Success Goal.
- Play longer games.
- Play higher-skilled players.

5. Game Point
[Corresponds to *Racquetball*, Step 18, Drill 3]

Group Management and Safety Tips

- Two players play per court.
- Others can chart serves or other shots while waiting their turns.

Equipment

- Charts
- Pencils

Instructions to Class

- "You are the receiver with the score 14-0 against you. Try to score 5 points before your opponent wins the game. This means you must take the serve away and score 5 points. If your opponent wins the game, reverse roles. No one expects you to win many of these games, but this will help you to overcome negative thoughts when you have game point against you."

Student Options

- "Change situation to 13-0, 12-0, etc."
- "Change game point to 7, 11, etc., and have score start at 6-0, 10-0, etc. If player gets within 2 points allow him or her to finish the game."
- "Create any score situation you wish."

Student Success Goal

- Score 5 points before your opponent wins the game.

To Decrease Difficulty

- Decrease the Success Goal.
- Have player who is behind serve the next point.
- Play player of lesser skill level.

To Increase Difficulty

- Increase the Success Goal.
- Play player of higher skill level.

6. Shot Selection Quiz (Oral Quiz)
[New Drill]

Group Management and Safety Tips

- This quiz could be used in a group setting or on an individual basis.
- The students will have a copy of the shot selection chart [Figure 18.1 in *Racquetball*, Step 18, Drill 4]. It would be best to have them take the quiz without using this chart.
- Ask two students to move to the positions that you describe.
- This drill is not an active one or one in which shots are hit.

Instructions to Class

- "When the two demonstrators move to the positions I describe, decide which shot (or shots) would be best for the player to hit. Raise your hand, and I will call on someone to list the shot or shots you would hit. Be prepared to explain your reasons. In most instances there may be more than one good choice."

Student Success Goal

- Have a correct choice for every situation presented.

To Decrease Difficulty

- Allow students to use shot selection chart [*Racquetball*, Step 18, Drill 4].

To Increase Difficulty

- Place a time limit on answers.
- Require that all correct possibilities be given.

Evaluation Ideas

Racquetball challenges the instructor who wishes to evaluate students thoroughly and fairly. One reason is that students come from a wide range of experiences and physical abilities. This is true in many other sports, but the nature of racquetball seems to amplify the differences. Students who have played some racquetball know the different bounces and angles the ball can take. They have an early advantage over the novice, who might never have seen the game played but who decided to take the course because someone has convinced him or her that racquetball is fun.

Because of these experience and ability ranges, you should incorporate both qualitative evaluations (form, style, or technique) and quantitative evaluations (number, performance, or amount) into your grading plan. While "proper" form is subject to interpretation and there have been many famous and successful exceptions to conventional form (Stan Musial in baseball, Dick Fosbury in high jump, and Parry O'Brien in shot put), in the early stages of learning, emphasis still should be on proper form and technique. So you need to evaluate your students on form, style, and technique. As one's skill level improves, the importance of performance (results) emerges and becomes more important.

Another factor should be considered in your overall grading plan: the balance between skills and knowledge. Often in physical education classes the psychomotor (physical skills) domain is emphasized to the exclusion or neglect of the cognitive domain (knowledge and understanding). You can evaluate subjectively your students' strategy and shot selection while you watch them play. Evaluating their knowledge can be done objectively through written tests.

You should decide the objectives in the psychomotor and cognitive areas, plan how these objectives will be assessed, and then tell students the plan at the beginning of the course. It is grossly unfair for the learner to attempt to learn objectives when the evaluation process is vague and may or may not include those objectives. Further, having a preconceived evaluation plan helps you teach in a more organized and focused manner.

QUANTITATIVE AND QUALITATIVE EVALUATION

In the short time you have with students, the novice will have little chance to catch or surpass the person who has moderate to extensive experience. Therefore, I recommend that you use both objective (quantitative) and subjective (qualitative) evaluations to measure student learning and progress.

If you choose subjective evaluation methods, you must be the evaluator: Beginning students are not experienced enough to evaluate qualitative performance accurately. Students also might be more generous than you to their friends and less fair to those they do not know or like.

Quantitative measures are less subjective, but to compare quantitative results (such as those obtained from the wall rally test), ensure that all tests are administered uniformly. Students and/ or assistants can be trained to administer such tests, but if time allows it is more consistent to have just one person administer them.

Size of class, number and location of courts, time available for testing, and proficiency of the evaluator will all affect how many different tests or evaluation methods are practical. Several specific methods are described for your consideration.

STUDENT SELF-EVALUATION

This self-evaluation method is outlined in *Racquetball: Steps to Success*. [See "Rating Your Total Progress," p. 141.] It is simple and easy to complete. Tell your students to use this chart to rate their own play. This method can be used in several ways. First, it can be an ongoing form of evaluation throughout the course. This would let the student know which skills to improve. Second, it can be used for summative evaluation at the end of the unit to show the student the extent of his or her progress. Third, it could be used at anytime for peer evaluation, which is of great value to both the evaluator and the person being evaluated. In all these cases, you may choose not to use the evaluation for grading purposes but instead as a gauge to show students their progress.

SUBJECTIVE TEACHER EVALUATION

You can use the same instrument to evaluate players subjectively as you watch them in a game. Again, you can decide whether to incorporate the results into the grading plan. A unique way to use this method is for the student to use the form for self-evaluation and the teacher to use the same form for subjective evaluation. (Mark it with a different colored pen or pencil.) You might even give a grade based on how accurately (by your measure) the student assessed himself or herself.

SKILL TESTING

You can use drills and forms from both the participant's book and the instructor's book to evaluate specific skills. For example, the detour zone chart (Step 13, Drill 3) and the service chart (Step 18, Drill 1) are two devices that can objectively measure progress in racquetball skills. Otherwise, you can record when students attain each drill's Success Goals as quantitative evidence of progress. You may or may not choose to utilize these measures in determining grades.

The 30-Second Wall Rally Test

If you wish to use only one skill test, consider the wall rally (Step 3, Drill 3). Many intangibles relate to winning racquetball games, but research has consistently shown a high correlation between this type of test and overall playing ability. Another name for this wall rally test could be the 30-second test. The score is the number of legal returns the player makes to the front wall in 30 seconds. Use Figure E.1 to record scores and also give you some norms that have been developed over the last 12 years with Augustana College students. You must follow some scoring rules if your results are to be meaningful when you compare your students' scores to the standards in the tables. Here are the rules:

- The ball must be dropped to the floor and hit upon its rebound to start the test.
- Do not start the clock until the player contacts the ball.
- All legal hits must be from behind the short line.
- Play the ball on the fly (volley) or after any number of bounces once the test starts.

- Count only legal returns to the front wall. For instance, a ball that hits the floor just before the front wall (skip) is not a legal return. This need not interrupt test continuity, however. Just do not add that one hit on the wall to the total; the player may continue without stopping.
- A ball that eludes the player toward the back wall may be played on any bounce. The player also may bring the ball back to the starting position before resuming the test.
- A player should quickly retrieve any ball that remains forward of the short line, and the test should be resumed from the original position. Or, the player has the option of waiting for the ball to roll back behind the short line if that would be better.
- Record the better of two trials. If the player does not reach a score of 3 before losing control of the ball, restart the test and don't count that effort as a trial.
- The player may use either forehand or backhand strokes to return the ball.

You may wish to use other rules when conducting this test, such as:

- Hand another ball to the player when he or she loses control of the ball.
- Allow more than two trials or limit the player to using only forehand or backhand.
- Use the average of two or three trials as the score.

Standards were based on the rules given, and any modifications you make also would require modifications of the standards.

There is room on the form in Figure E.1 for multiple testing results. I suggest that you administer this test when covering Step 3 and one or two more times during the unit. This is an excellent drill for developing racquet control. Students will be especially motivated to practice this drill if it is part of the overall grading plan and announced as such early in the unit. Over time, you should use your students' results from this testing to create your own set of norms.

FUNNEL TOURNAMENT

Playing in a tournament helps measure performance and adds excitement and interest at a time students are ready for it. The ideal time to introduce tournament play is about two-thirds

30-second wall rally test

Name	Date		Date		Date	
	Trial 1	Trial 2	Trial 1	Trial 2	Trial 1	Trial 2

Male		Female		
HS-Jr High	College	HS-Jr High	College	Rating
0-7	0-9	0-5	0-7	Need practice
8-12	10-14	6-10	8-12	Fair
13-17	15-19	11-15	13-17	Good
18-up	20-up	16-up	18-up	Excellent

Figure E.1 30-second wall rally testing chart.

of the way through the course. You will see a rapid spurt in improvement when students start to play games that have more meaning. Be careful not to reward the experienced player or penalize the novice who, in a few weeks, may not be able to make up the difference in abilities. The funnel tournament and accompanying rules presented in Figure E.2 outline a way to give students a fair opportunity for competition. It allows players to play others very near to their ability levels and yet challenges players at a higher level. It does not force the low-ability student to play the high-ability student as do many tournaments.

The funnel tournament can be modified to fit different class sizes and ability ranges. You may wish to divide your class into two or three tournaments with participants flighted by ability or individual choice. The 30-second wall rally test would be an ideal way to determine students' ability levels in large classes.

The funnel tournament is flexible in terms of time required: It can be continued for as many days as you feel is necessary. The tournament also can accommodate different sizes of groups by adding or subtracting levels on the upper or lower ends.

This funnel tournament can be incorporated into your grading plan. One option is to base part of your students' grades upon their position after the final day of tournament play. This tends to favor more experienced players, but it is surprising that by the end of the course many novices have caught up with those who were more experienced at the start. A second option is to award grades based upon the total number of points accumulated (Figure E.2). This is fair to all because everyone has the same chance to earn points. In fact, those lower in the standings have a slightly easier time accumulating points. A third option for grading would be to use a combination of the first two options.

Funnel Tournament

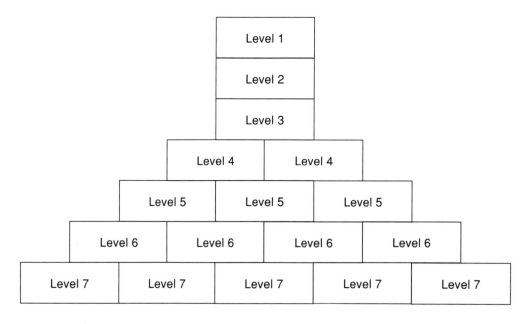

Rules for Play   1. A player can challenge only one level above him or her. Exceptions: Level 4 could challenge Levels 2 or 3. Level 3 could challenge Levels 2 or 1.
2. A challenge from below must be honored before a second upward challenge.
3. If you challenge upward and defeat someone, you move up and they move down.
4. Upward challenges are optional; you may play at your own level as much as you wish.

Point Totals   You can incorporate a point system for this tournament if you wish. Points can be awarded as follows:
2 points for winning a game
1 point for losing a game
1 bonus point if the victory or loss was an upward challenge

Figure E.2   Funnel tournament diagram.

KNOWLEDGE TEST

A knowledge test should be included in the grading plan for every activity class, including racquetball. Knowledge of strategy, rules, techniques, and safety are important objectives, and can be assessed effectively by written knowledge tests.

The "Test Bank" section contains 81 test questions about rules, strokes, fundamentals, and strategy. It would be appropriate for testing students' knowledge of the material presented in class and in their text. Select questions from this bank or formulate your own questions according to your needs.

Test Bank

These questions cover racquetball rules, techniques, and strategy. Select those that test material taught in your course. Consider the length and depth of your instructional period and the levels of your learners when selecting questions. You may wish to modify or add items to reflect the emphasis in your instructional techniques and philosophy.

RULES

Directions: Place the letter corresponding to the correct answer for each question in the blank provided.

_____ 1. A player attempts to serve but misses the ball completely. What is the ruling?
   a. an out
   b. dead ball
   c. no penalty; player serves again
   d. fault
   e. none of the above

_____ 2. A hinder is
   a. a hard serve
   b. a bad player
   c. a service that completely eludes the receiver
   d. a type of interference in play

_____ 3. Before each service, the server calls out
   a. his or her score
   b. his or her opponent's score
   c. both scores with his or her score first
   d. both scores with his or her opponent's score first

_____ 4. Cutthroat is
   a. three people in a court, all against each other
   b. five in court
   c. three against two
   d. playing by yourself

_____ 5. Stepping over the service line or short line in the act of serving would be classified as
   a. a hinder
   b. a fault
   c. an out
   d. a replay

_____ 6. When serving, a ball that strikes the side wall before hitting the front wall is termed
   a. a fault
   b. a hinder
   c. an out
   d. a dead ball

_____ 7. A serve
   a. must hit front wall first
   b. can hit right side wall first
   c. can hit left side wall first
   d. can hit floor or ceiling first

_____ 8. A *kill* is

    a. a shot hit so low on the front wall that it is impossible to return
    b. a hinder that results in physical injury
    c. a returned ball that, upon rebound, gets past the opponent
    d. a service that strikes the opponent in the air

_____ 9. What is the term for a service that can't be returned?

    a. ace
    b. crotch ball
    c. dead ball
    d. smash

_____ 10. A common game played by three players is

    a. three musketeers
    b. triangles
    c. cutthroat
    d. doubles

_____ 11. Official racquetball games are played to

    a. 7 points
    b. 15 points
    c. 21 points
    d. 10 points

_____ 12. To win a racquetball game

    a. you must be ahead by 4 points at the end
    b. you must be ahead by 3 points at the end
    c. you must be ahead by 2 points at the end
    d. you must be ahead by 1 point at the end

_____ 13. When returning the serve, the receiver

    a. must play the ball in the air
    b. must play the ball before the second bounce
    c. may play the ball after any number of bounces
    d. may play the ball after two bounces

_____ 14. To score a point, the receiver

    a. must win the rally
    b. must hit a kill shot
    c. must take the service away from the server with a passing shot
    d. all of the above
    e. none of the above

_____ 15. The line 5 feet in front of the short line is the

    a. receiving line
    b. service line
    c. no passing line
    d. 5-foot line

_____ 16. A service that hits the floor before reaching the front wall is

    a. a fault
    b. a hinder
    c. an out
    d. a short serve

_____ 17. If the server leaves the service zone before the served ball crosses the short line on the fly it is

    a. a good idea
    b. an out
    c. a point for the receiver
    d. a foot fault

_____ 18. In serving, the server may stand
  a. in front of the service line
  b. behind the short line
  c. with either foot over the short line
  d. anywhere between the short line and service line
  e. none of the above

_____ 19. During play, the ball is swung at and missed. What is the ruling?
  a. rally is over
  b. ball still in play
  c. dead ball
  d. automatic point
  e. none of the above

_____ 20. The receiver may play the serve
  a. only after it crosses the receiving line or bounces on the floor behind the short line
  b. anytime
  c. after it crosses the short line
  d. all of the above
  e. none of the above

_____ 21. A served ball hits the front wall, then the ceiling, then the floor behind the short line. What is the ruling?
  a. legal serve
  b. out
  c. fault
  d. ceiling shot

_____ 22. Player A attempts to return the ball to the front wall. It strikes player B and continues on to hit the front wall. What is the ruling?
  a. ball is in play
  b. hinder
  c. point for player A
  d. point for player B

_____ 23. Player A blocks the ball from player B's sight, making it impossible for B to return the ball. What is the ruling?
  a. point for player B
  b. point for player A
  c. hinder
  d. dead ball

_____ 24. A served ball rebounds to hit the back wall before hitting the floor. What is the ruling?
  a. receiver has option to play the serve or not
  b. out
  c. fault
  d. dead ball
  e. legal serve; ball is in play

_____ 25. A crotch serve (which hits the front wall and side wall at the same time) is
  a. an out
  b. a fault
  c. a dead ball
  d. none of the above

_____ 26. A served ball hits the ceiling before the front wall. What is the ruling?
  a. out
  b. fault
  c. dead ball
  d. depends upon where the ball lands

_____ 27. Player A returns the ball toward the front wall. It hits player B, but is traveling so slowly it would not have reached the front wall. What is the ruling?
  a. hinder
  b. player A loses the rally
  c. player B loses the rally
  d. none of the above

_____ 28. A ball in play goes directly from the front wall to a screen on the back wall. What is the ruling?
  a. point for player who hit it
  b. point against player who hit it
  c. ball is still in play
  d. court hinder

_____ 29. A served ball touching the server directly from the front wall is
  a. an out
  b. a fault
  c. a dead ball
  d. in play

_____ 30. The server steps on but not over the short line while serving. What is the ruling?
  a. foot fault
  b. out
  c. dead ball
  d. legal serve

_____ 31. A *short* is
  a. an out
  b. small player
  c. a fault on a serve
  d. failure to return the ball to the front wall

_____ 32. The server serves two *longs* in a row. What is the ruling?
  a. server is out
  b. receiver scores 1 point
  c. server gets one more try
  d. both a and b

_____ 33. The server must hit the ball
  a. anytime
  b. after one bounce
  c. after two bounces
  d. before it bounces

_____ 34. The serve hits the front wall and both side walls before hitting the floor. What is the ruling?
  a. depends upon where the ball hits the floor
  b. fault
  c. out
  d. point for the receiver

_____ 35. During the serve, the receiver must stand
  a. anywhere on the court
  b. behind the service line
  c. behind the receiving line
  d. behind the short line and in front of the receiving line

_____ 36. Under which circumstances must the play be repeated?
  a. an error
  b. a fault
  c. a kill
  d. a hinder

_____ 37. Which of the following is an *out* serve?
  a. ball lands on short line
  b. ball hits receiver's body
  c. serve hits two side walls
  d. serve hitting ceiling before hitting front wall

STROKES AND FUNDAMENTALS

Directions: Place the letter corresponding to the correct answer for each question in the blank provided.

_____ 1. Where should the V formed by the thumb and forefinger be on the Eastern backhand grip?
  a. top back bevel
  b. top front bevel
  c. top center of handle
  d. none of the above

_____ 2. To serve a good power serve, you must
  a. swing fast and hard
  b. transfer weight smoothly
  c. keep your knees straight
  d. bounce the ball high
  e. all of the above

_____ 3. To learn to play the back wall, one should
  a. pivot with the ball
  b. don't chase it; go to meet it
  c. stay near the midline
  d. wait for the ball to drop
  e. all of the above
  f. none of the above

_____ 4. The most important element of a kill shot is to
  a. hit it hard
  b. hit it to their backhand
  c. use it sparingly
  d. keep it low

_____ 5. In cutthroat,
  a. the server must hit better shots to score points
  b. the receivers have a better chance to return the serve
  c. shot selection for the server is more important
  d. all of the above
  e. none of the above

_____ 6. The hard Z-serve is difficult to execute because
  a. the starting position is difficult
  b. the receiver has the advantage
  c. the service zone is not large enough
  d. more power is required

_____ 7. The Z-shot is easier to hit than the Z-serve because
  a. it does not have to hit the floor between hits on the side walls
  b. it is usually hit with a backhand stroke
  c. it is usually hit when returning a low shot
  d. it does not have to be hit as hard

_____ 8. A proper warm-up includes
   a. cardiovascular exercises
   b. stretching exercises
   c. progressive hitting
   d. all of the above
   e. none of the above

_____ 9. The way you grip the racquet is of concern to
   a. all players
   b. experts only
   c. beginners only
   d. intermediate players

_____ 10. The advantage of the Continental grip is
   a. it is easier to learn
   b. it is the most efficient
   c. it is the most popular
   d. all of the above
   e. none of the above

_____ 11. Important fundamentals about the grip are
   a. the racquet should be held deep in the palm of the hand
   b. the fingers should grip the racquet tightly at all times
   c. one should grip the racquet as close to the end or butt of the handle as possible
   d. all of the above
   e. none of the above

_____ 12. A left-handed player hitting a forehand stroke can direct the ball to his or her right side by having the racquet face
   a. closed
   b. square
   c. open
   d. all of the above
   e. none of the above

_____ 13. A right-handed player can direct a forehand shot upward (side view) by having the racquet face
   a. closed
   b. square
   c. open
   d. all of the above
   e. none of the above

_____ 14. A right-handed player can cause the racquet face to close (top view) when hitting a backhand shot by contacting the ball
   a. in front of the front hip
   b. even with the front hip
   c. behind the front hip
   d. none of the above

_____ 15. The beginner's power serve should use the same mechanics as the
   a. backhand stroke
   b. forehand stroke
   c. overhead stroke
   d. underhand stroke

_____ 16. The serve used much less than it should be is the
   a. power serve
   b. lob serve
   c. hard Z-serve
   d. soft Z-serve
   e. none of the above

_____ 17. Which is *not* a big concern when serving a down-the-line lob serve?
   a. The serve might hit the side wall first.
   b. The server must remember to move to center court.
   c. The serve is easy to return with a kill shot.
   d. The serve may hit the side wall when rebounding and come out toward the middle of the court.
   e. all of the above
   f. none of the above

_____ 18. The differences between the beginner's power serve and the power serve are
   a. power serve is usually lower and harder
   b. server must move with power serve
   c. beginner's serve is easier to execute
   d. all of the above
   e. none of the above

_____ 19. The top reason for the inability to return power serves is
   a. a poor grip
   b. failure to watch the ball
   c. poor receiving position
   d. lack of confidence

_____ 20. The position for hitting a ceiling shot can best be compared to
   a. a catcher in softball ready to catch a pitch
   b. a basketball player guarding someone dribbling the ball
   c. a soccer goalie trying to block a scoring shot
   d. a baseball outfielder ready to catch a fly ball
   e. all of the above
   f. none of the above

STRATEGY

Directions: Place the letter corresponding to the correct answer for each question in the blank provided.

_____ 1. When you are deep against the back wall and your opponent is in the left court in front of the service line your best shot would be to attempt a
   a. ceiling shot
   b. kill shot
   c. passing shot
   d. pick-up shot

_____ 2. When your opponent is fairly deep and behind you, it is a good time to execute a
   a. ceiling shot
   b. kill shot
   c. passing shot
   d. pick-up shot

_____ 3. The best thing for a receiver of the serve to remember is
  a. watch the opponent
  b. watch the wall
  c. watch the ball
  d. watch the opponent's feet
  e. all of the above
  f. none of the above

_____ 4. A ceiling shot
  a. is called a hinder under AARA rules
  b. results in point or side-out for the player or team that executes it
  c. is used to make the opponent move out of the center court position
  d. is generally a better shot against a short player

_____ 5. When your opponent is in front of you, the best shot to use would be a
  a. passing shot
  b. kill shot
  c. around-the-wall shot
  d. Z-shot

_____ 6. Which of the following is the _single_ most important skill in a good racquetball player?
  a. control of shots
  b. powerful serve
  c. aggressive personality
  d. variety of serves

_____ 7. The center court position is
  a. important only in cutthroat
  b. not important
  c. important at all times
  d. important only for the server

_____ 8. Upon reaching center court a player should
  a. check over his or her shoulder often
  b. watch the opponent at all times
  c. relax, because he or she probably will win the point
  d. anticipate the opponent's return

_____ 9. Which shot is an offensive shot?
  a. around-the-wall shot
  b. lob shot
  c. Z-shot
  d. pinch kill

_____ 10. Which shot is the poorest choice when your opponent is in the front court?
  a. lob shot
  b. ceiling shot
  c. passing shot
  d. kill shot

_____ 11. You should serve to your opponent's backhand because
  a. it is a rule
  b. he or she prefers it
  c. that is generally the weaker shot
  d. none of the above
  e. all of the above

____ 12. The best serve to use against a power player is
    a. power serve
    b. lob serve
    c. Z-serve
    d. combination of a, b, and c

____ 13. The most basic shot during play is the
    a. passing shot
    b. ceiling shot
    c. kill shot
    d. Z-shot

____ 14. The main purpose of the ceiling shot is to
    a. score a point
    b. tire your opponent
    c. make your opponent use the backhand
    d. make your opponent vacate center court

____ 15. When should you purposely let the ball go to the back wall?
    a. whenever necessary
    b. whenever it would be playable
    c. never
    d. all the time

____ 16. The main purpose of a kill shot is to
    a. end the rally
    b. tire your opponent
    c. make your opponent use the backhand
    d. draw your opponent up front

____ 17. The purpose of the detour zone rule is to help you
    a. plan the type of shots you hit
    b. plan the location of your shots
    c. decorate the court
    d. consider the location of your opponent
    e. all of the above
    f. none of the above

____ 18. The detour zone rule applies to
    a. kill shots
    b. ceiling shots
    c. passing shots
    d. Z-shots
    e. all of the above
    f. none of the above

____ 19. The up-and-back formation in cutthroat is weak against
    a. kill shots
    b. ceiling shots
    c. Z-shots
    d. passing shots

____ 20. The Z-serves are important because
    a. they add to the variety of serves you have
    b. they are the only safe serves to someone's forehand
    c. they are usually good for aces
    d. all of the above
    e. none of the above

_____ 21. The hard Z-serve is hard to return because
   a. it is very high
   b. it is hard to follow
   c. it rebounds from the wall at an unusual angle
   d. all of the above
   e. none of the above

_____ 22. The best return of a soft Z-serve from the rear corner is a
   a. kill shot
   b. ceiling shot
   c. passing shot
   d. Z-shot

_____ 23. The best return of a hard Z-serve is generally a
   a. kill shot
   b. passing shot
   c. ceiling shot
   d. Z-shot

_____ 24. Hitting the ball into the back wall to return it to the front wall
   a. should never be done
   b. is a good idea
   c. puts extra spin on the ball
   d. requires a high level of skill

ANSWERS TO TEST QUESTIONS

Rules		Strokes and Fundamentals	Strategy
1. a	27. b	1. a	1. c
2. d	28. d	2. b	2. b
3. c	29. a	3. e	3. c
4. a	30. d	4. d	4. c
5. b	31. c	5. d	5. a
6. c	32. a	6. d	6. a
7. a	33. b	7. a	7. c
8. a	34. b	8. d	8. d
9. a	35. c	9. a	9. d
10. c	36. d	10. a	10. d
11. b	37. d	11. e	11. c
12. d		12. a	12. b
13. b		13. c	13. a
14. e		14. a	14. d
15. b		15. b	15. b
16. c		16. b	16. a
17. d		17. c	17. b
18. d		18. d	18. e
19. b		19. c	19. d
20. a		20. d	20. a
21. c			21. c
22. b			22. b
23. c			23. b
24. c			24. a
25. a			
26. a			

Appendix A
How to Use the Knowledge Structure (Overview)

By completing an instructional tool called a knowledge structure you make a personal statement about what you know about a subject and how that knowledge guides your teaching and coaching decisions. The Knowledge Structure of Racquetball outlined in Figure A.1 is designed for a teaching environment and includes progressions that emphasize technique and performance objectives in realistic settings. In a coaching environment, you might need to emphasize more physiological and conditioning factors and include progressions that prepare athletes for competition.

The Knowledge Structure of Racquetball shows the first page or an **overview** of a completed knowledge structure. The knowledge structure is divided into broad categories of information that are used for all participant and instructor guides in the Steps to Success Activity Series. Those categories are

- physiological training and conditioning,
- background knowledge,
- psychomotor skills and strategies, and
- psychosocial concepts.

Physiological training and conditioning has several subcategories, including warm-up and cool-down. Research in exercise physiology and the medical sciences shows clearly the importance of warming up before and cooling down after physical activity. The participant and instructor guides present principles and exercises for effective warm-up and cool-down, which, because of time restrictions, are usually the only training activities done in the teaching environment. In a more intense coaching environment, categories should be added—training principles, injury prevention, training progressions, and nutrition principles.

The background-knowledge category presents subcategories of information that represent essential background knowledge that all instructors should command when meeting their classes. For racquetball, background knowledge includes playing the game, basic rules, equipment, and safety.

Under the heading psychomotor skill and strategies, all individual skills in an activity are named. For racquetball, these are ball control, serves and returns, passing shots, ceiling shots, kill shots, Z-shots, and around-the-wall shots. These skills are listed in a recommended order of presentation. In a completed knowledge structure, each skill is broken down into subskills, delineating selected technical, biomechanical, motor learning, and other teaching and coaching points that describe mature performance. These points can be found in the Student Keys to Success Checklists in the participant's book.

A unique feature of this book is that tactics are integrated into the learning process as the skills are presented. This interrelationship of technique and tactic develops good habits: the proper strategy applied to the appropriate technique. Hitting to an opponent's backhand, gaining a center court advantage, playing the back wall, shot placement, and adjusting to game conditions are all integrated into the learning process at appropriate times—and earlier than in other approaches.

The psychosocial category identifies selected concepts from sports psychology and sociology literature that have been shown to contribute to the learner's understanding of and success in the activity. Successful approaches are built into the key concepts and activities for teaching. For racquetball, the concept identified is decision making.

To be a successful teacher or coach, you must convert what you have learned as a student or achieved as a performer into knowledge that helps others learn. A knowledge structure is a tool designed to help you with this transition and to help you and your students achieve success quicker. You should view a knowledge structure as the most basic level of teaching knowledge you possess for a sport or activity. For more information on how to develop your own knowledge structure, see the textbook that accompanies this series, *Instructional Design for Teaching Physical Activities* (Vickers, 1990).

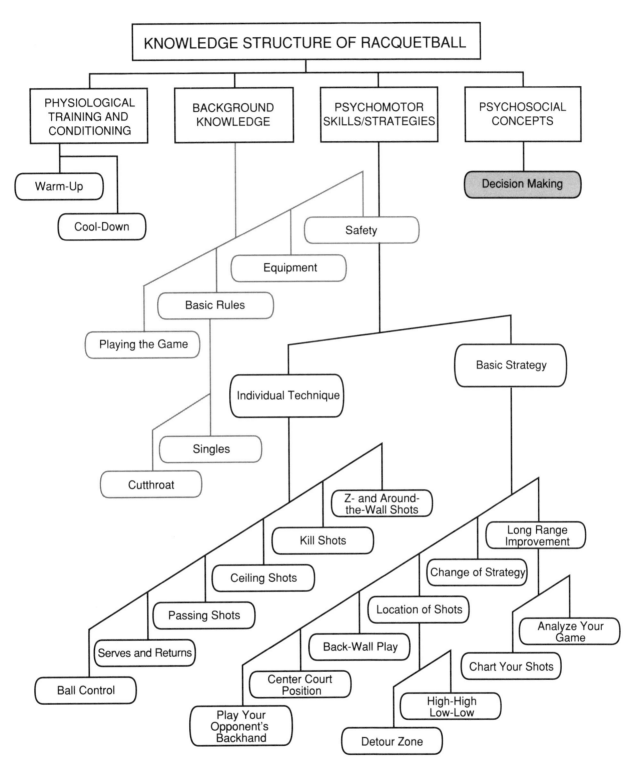

Figure A.1   Knowledge structure of racquetball.

Appendix B.1
How to Use the Scope and Teaching Sequence Form

A completed Scope and Teaching Sequence form is, in effect, a master lesson plan. It lists all the individual skills to be included in your course, recorded (vertically) in the progressive sequence in which you have decided to present them showing (horizontally) the manner and the session in which you plan to teach them.

The sample Scope and Teaching Sequence form (Appendix B.1) illustrates how the chart might be used in a 28-meeting, semester-long course. This chart indicates that ceiling shots will be introduced in session 9. It also indicates that Step 3 skills (forehand and backhand) are worked on for two sessions—one introduction and one review.

A course Scope and Teaching Sequence chart (Appendix B.2) will help you to plan your daily teaching strategies better. (See Appendix D.1.) It will take some experience to predict accurately how much material you can cover in each session, but by completing a plan like this, you can compare your progress to your next plan and revise the plan to better fit the next class.

The chart also will help you tailor the amount of material to the length of time you have to teach it. Be sure that your course's Scope and Teaching Sequence allots ample time for review and practice of each area.

Sample Scope and Teaching Sequence

New [N]   Review [R]   Continue [C]

NAME OF ACTIVITY _____

LEVEL OF LEARNER _____

Steps	Session Number	1	2	3	4	5	6	7	8	9	10	11	12	13	14	15	16	17	18	19	20	21	22	23	24	25	26	27	28	29	30
	Introduction	N																													
1	The grips		N	R																											
2	Developing ball control		N	R	R																										
3	Forehand & backhand			N	R																										
4	Beginner's power serve					N	C											R													
5	Rule #1—Hit to their backhand					N	C											R													
6	Lob serve						N	C																							
7	Power serve							N										R													
8	Rule #2—I own center court							N	C																						
9	Passing shots								N	R																					
10	Ceiling shots									N	R							R													
11	Rule #3—Love the back wall										N	R																			
12	Kill shots											N	R																		
13	Rule #4—Detour zone												N	R				R													
14	Cutthroat													N																	
15	Z-serves														N	R															
16	Rule #5—High-high; low-low															N	R														
17	Z- and around-the-wall shots																N														
18	Rule #6—Never change a winning game; always change a losing game																	N													
	Tournament play																			N	C	C	C	C	C	C	C	C	C		
	Wall rally skill test																										N	C	C		
	Written test																		N	R											

Appendix B.2

Scope and Teaching Sequence

NAME OF ACTIVITY _____

LEVEL OF LEARNER _____

New N   Feview R   Continue C

Session Number →

Steps	1	2	3	4	5	6	7	8	9	10	11	12	13	14	15	16	17	18	19	20	21	22	23	24	25	26	27	28	29	30

Note. From *Badminton: A Structures of Knowledge Approach* (pp. 60-61) by J.N. Vickers and D. Brecht, 1987, Calgary, AB: University Printing Services. Copyright 1987 by Joan N. Vickers. Adapted by permission.

Appendix C.1
How to Use the Individual Program Form

To complete an individual program for each student, you must first make five decisions about evaluation:

1. How many skills or concepts can you or should you evaluate, considering the number of students and the time available? The larger your classes and the shorter your class length, the fewer objectives you will be able to use.
2. What specific quantitative or qualitative criteria will you use to evaluate specific skills? See the Sample Individual Program (Appendix C.1) for ideas.
3. What relative weight is to be assigned to each skill, considering its importance in the course and the amount of practice time available?
4. What type of grading system do you wish to use? Will you use letters (A, B, C, D); satisfactory/unsatisfactory; a number or point system (1, 2, 3); or percentages (10 percent, 20 percent, 30 percent)? Or you may prefer a system of achievement levels, such as colors (red, white, blue); creatures (panthers, lions, tigers); or medallions (gold, silver, bronze).
5. Who will do the evaluating? You may want to delegate certain quantitative evaluations to be made by the students' peers up to a predetermined skill level (e.g., a B grade), and reserve all qualitative evaluations and all top-grade determinations for yourself.

Once you have made these decisions, draw up an evaluation sheet (using Appendix C.2) that fits most of your class members. Then decide whether you will establish a minimum level as a passing/failing point. Calculate the minimum passing score and the maximum attainable score, and divide the difference into as many grade categories as you wish. If you use an achievement-level system, assign a numerical value to each level for your calculations.

The blank Individual Program form, as shown in Appendix C.2, is intended not to be used verbatim (although you may if you wish), but rather to suggest ideas that you can use, adapt, and integrate with your own ideas to tailor your program to you and your students. One modification for working with large groups is to reduce the number of technique and performance objectives to be evaluated.

Make copies of your own program evaluation system to hand out to each student at your first class meeting and be prepared to make modifications for those who need special consideration. Some modifications: changing the weight assigned to particular skills for certain students, or substituting some skills for others, or varying the criteria used for evaluating selected students. This lets you recognize individual differences within your class.

You, the instructor, have the freedom to make the decisions about evaluating your students. Be creative. The best teachers always are.

Sample Individual Program

INDIVIDUAL COURSE IN _____ Racquetball _____ GRADE/COURSE SECTION _____

STUDENT'S NAME _____ STUDENT ID # _____

SKILLS/CONCEPTS	TECHNIQUE AND PERFORMANCE OBJECTIVES	WT* %	POINT PROGRESS**				FINAL SCORE*** =
			1 D	2 C	3 B	4 A	
1 Ready position	*Technique:* Racquet and weight forward; knees slightly bent; head and shoulders facing front wall; weight on balls of both feet	1					
2 Forehand grip	*Technique:* "V" of thumb and forefinger on top back corner bevel	1					
3 Forehand stroke	*Technique:* Start backswing early, weight on back foot, body facing side wall, eyes focused on ball; swing through ball; control ball; transfer weight; follow through; recover quickly	1					
	Performance: Complete 30-second wall rally test using forehand strokes only	2	1-10	11-12	13-15	15+	
4 Backhand grip	*Technique:* "V" of thumb and forefinger on top back corner bevel	1					
5 Backhand stroke	*Technique:* Start backswing early, weight on back foot, body facing side wall, eyes focused on ball; stroke ball smoothly; control ball; transfer weight; follow through; recover quickly	1					
	Performance: Complete 30-second wall rally test using backhand strokes only	2	1-5	6-8	9-10	10+	
6 Beginner's power serve	*Technique:* Forehand grip; controlled swing; eyes on ball; good weight transfer; recover balance; move to center court	1					
	Performance: Serve 10 times to backhand side of court	2	1-3	4-5	6-8	9-10	

| SKILLS/CONCEPTS | TECHNIQUE AND PERFORMANCE OBJECTIVES | WT* % | × | POINT PROGRESS** | | | = | FINAL SCORE*** |
			1 D	2 C	3 B	4 A		
7 Lob serve	*Technique:* Good ball bounce; smooth swing; subtle weight transfer; soft touch; move to center court	1						
	Performance: 10 serves to backhand side of court	2	1-3	4-5	6-8	9-10		
8 Passing shots	*Performance:* From behind short line, hit 8 consecutive down-the-line forehand passing shots that do not hit side wall	2	1-2	3-4	5-6	7-8		
9 Ceiling shots	*Performance:* Playing behind the short line, keep the ball in play for 8 consecutive ceiling shots using either forehand or backhand	2	1-2	3-4	5-6	7-8		
10 Kill shots	*Performance:* Hit 10 kill shots from paper cup at short line; ball must contact floor twice before reaching service line	3	1-2	3-5	6-7	8-10		
11 Z-serve (soft)	*Performance:* Hit 10 legal soft Z-serves that rebound no more than 5 feet from the back wall and die in the backhand corner	2	1-2	3-5	6-7	8-10		
12 Game play	*Technique:* Get to ball early; good setup; smooth strokes; use strategy rules 1-6; recover quickly to center court; anticipate opponent's return	2						
	Performance: Compete in funnel tournament							

*WT = Weighting of an objective's degree of difficulty.

**PROGRESS = Ongoing success, which may be expressed in terms of (a) accumulated points (1, 2, 3, 4); (b) grades (D, C, B, A); (c) symbols (merit, bronze, silver, gold); (d) unsatisfactory/satisfactory; and others as desired.

***FINAL SCORE equals WT times PROGRESS.

Appendix C.2

Individual Program

INDIVIDUAL COURSE IN _____

GRADE/COURSE SECTION _____

STUDENT'S NAME _____

STUDENT ID # _____

SKILLS/CONCEPTS	TECHNIQUE AND PERFORMANCE OBJECTIVES	WT* %	×	POINT PROGRESS** 1	2	3	4	=	FINAL SCORE***

Note. From "The Role of Expert Knowledge Structures in an Instructional Design Model for Physical Education" by J.N. Vickers, 1983, *Journal of Teaching in Physical Education,* **2**(3), p. 17. Copyright 1983 by Joan N. Vickers. Adapted by permission.

*WT = Weighting of an objective's degree of difficulty.

**PROGRESS = Ongoing success, which may be expressed in terms of (a) accumulated points (1, 2, 3, 4); (b) grades (D, C, B, A); (c) symbols (merit, bronze, silver, gold); (d) unsatisfactory/satisfactory; and others as desired.

***FINAL SCORE equals WT times PROGRESS.

Appendix D.1
How to Use the Lesson Plan Form

All teachers have been trained that lesson plans are vital to good teaching. This is an axiom, but lesson plans can take many forms.

An effective lesson plan sets forth the objectives to be attained or attempted during the session. If there is no objective, there is no reason for teaching and no basis for judging whether the teaching is effective.

Once you have itemized your objectives, list specific activities that will lead to attaining each. Every activity must be described in detail: what will take place and in what order, and how the class will be organized for optimum learning. Record key phrases as focal points and as brief reminders of applicable safety precautions. For example, tell your students not to collide with their courtmates, to beware of racquetballs in flight and racquets being swung, and not to look back if they are in front of someone who is hitting.

Finally, to guide you in keeping to your plan, set a time schedule that allocates a segment of the lesson for each activity. Include in your lesson plan a list of all teaching and safety equipment you will need, and a reminder to check before class for availability and location of the equipment.

An organized, professional approach to teaching requires daily lesson plans. Each lesson plan provides you an effective overview of your intended instruction and a means to evaluate it when class is over. And having lesson plans on file allows someone else to teach in your absence.

You may modify the blank Lesson Plan form shown in Appendix D.2 to fit your needs, just as I have modified it in the sample (Appendix D.1) to include an equipment list.

Sample Lesson Plan

LESSON PLAN __2__ OF __28__		OBJECTIVES:	
ACTIVITY _____ Beginning Racquetball _____		1. Students will learn and demonstrate the Eastern forehand and backhand grips and also the Continental grip.	
CLASS _____		2. Students will learn and practice drills to improve control of ball with racquet.	
EQUIPMENT _ One racquet and one ball per _		3. Students will practice wall rally drill.	
_____ student _____			

SKILL OR CONCEPT	LEARNING ACTIVITIES	TEACHING POINTS	TIME (MIN)
1. Outline objectives of today's class, also review starting time for class.	1. Announcements.	1. Remind students of time to be ready.	1
2. Proper warm-up.	2. Group warm-up (see *Racquetball*, pp. 9-13).	2. Students will be responsible for warm-up on own after 3rd meeting. Start slowly—warm-up gradually, stretch—don't bounce.	8
3. Demonstrate and check Eastern forehand grip.	3. Students work in pairs, check grip of partner (see Step 1, Drill 2).	3. "V" of thumb and forefinger on top back bevel. Mark bevel with chalk. Mark "V" with washable marker.	3
4. Demonstrate and check Eastern backhand grip.	4. Continue Step 1, Drill 2 with partner. Change grips back and forth.	4. "V" should be centered on top back bevel.	3
5. Demonstrate and check Continental grip.	5. Continue Step 1, Drill 2 "Shake hands" concept.	5. Remind students of other factors: Finger control, tension, pointing racquet at target.	3
6. Different "feel" of incorrect grip.	6. Frying pan grip (see Step 1, Drill 1).	6. Have students try forehand and backhand swings to feel how awkward the incorrect grip feels.	2
7. Racquet control.	7. Demonstrate floor dribbles and air dribbles (see Step 2, Drill 1).	7. Spread out—eye on ball—work on touch—hit ball softly with control.	6
8. Racquet control, angle control, wall rally.	8. Wall rally (see Step 2, Drill 2).	8. Demonstrate, then send students to "home" courts to practice. Remind them to check their grip.	10
9. Angle control.	9. Angle control drill (see Step 2, Drill 3).	9. Visit courts or call students together. Review angle of racquet and its effect on ball direction. Concentrate on proper body position with regard to ball.	10
10. Closure.	10. Review of lesson, announcements, bridge to next lesson.	10. Call students together. Ask for questions. Review drill and concept. Assign Step 3 for next time. Cool-down not necessary this time.	4

Appendix D.2

Lesson Plan

LESSON PLAN _____ OF _____		OBJECTIVES:	
ACTIVITY _____			
CLASS _____			
SKILL OR CONCEPT	LEARNING ACTIVITIES	TEACHING POINTS	TIME (MIN)

Note. From *Badminton: A Structures of Knowledge Approach* (p. 95) by J.N. Vickers and D. Brecht, 1987, Calgary, AB: University Printing Services. Copyright 1987 by Joan N. Vickers. Reprinted by permission.

References

Arbogast, G., & Lavay, B. (1987). Combining students with different ability levels in games and sports. *Physical Educator*, **44**(1), 225-260.

Belka, D. (1983). Racquetballers: Put yourself in the driver's seat. *Journal of Physical Education, Recreation and Dance*, **54**(5), 31.

Goc-Karp, G., & Zakrajsek, D.B. (1987). Planning for learning: Theory into practice. *Journal of Teaching in Physical Education*, **6**(4), 377-392.

Housner, L.D., & Griffey, D.C. (1985). Teacher cognition: Differences in planning and interactive decision making between experienced and inexperienced teachers. *Research Quarterly for Exercise and Sport*, **56**(1), 45-53.

Imwold, C.H., & Hoffman, S.J. (1983). Visual recognition of a gymnastic skill by experienced and inexperienced instructors. *Research Quarterly for Exercise and Sport*, **54**(2), 149-155.

Maughan, R.J. (1989). Optional games for racquetball classes. *Journal of Physical Education, Recreation and Dance*, **60**(6), 24-28.

Meacci, W.C., Pastore, D., & Karwoski, J. (1989). Racquetball: Teaching killshots to a novice. *Strategies*, **2**(3), 26-27.

Peterson, Alan P. (1989). Skill assessment for college racquetball classes. *Journal of Physical Education, Recreation and Dance*, **60**(4), 71-73.

Pizzaro, D.C., & Schott, R. (1990). The racquetball error shot chart—Learning and teaching aid. *Journal of Physical Education, Recreation and Dance*, **61**(1), 19-22.

Stewart, C.C. (1987). Teaching beginners in racquetball. Ideas on individualization. *Journal of Physical Education, Recreation and Dance*, **58**(4), 24-25.

Strand, B. (1988). Seven strategies to extend your racquetball course. *Journal of Physical Education, Recreation and Dance*, **59**(1), 19-21.

Vickers, J.N. (1990). *Instructional design for teaching physical activities*. Champaign, IL: Human Kinetics.

Vinger, P.F. (1983). Eye protection for racquet sports. *Journal of Physical Education, Recreation and Dance*, **54**(6), 46-48.

Ziegler, S.G. (1987). Negative thought stopping. A key to performance enhancement. *Journal of Physical Education, Recreation and Dance*, **58**(4), 66-69.

About the Author

Stan Kittleson is an accomplished racquetball player—he has taught the sport since 1972 and has been a physical educator in college settings since 1968. A professor of physical education at Augustana College in Rock Island, Illinois, Dr. Kittleson earned his PhD from the University of Illinois in 1973. He has served as president of the Illinois Association for Professional Preparation in Health, Physical Education, and Recreation and is a member of the American Alliance for Health, Physical Education, Recreation and Dance. When not teaching or playing racquetball, Dr. Kittleson enjoys scuba diving, alpine skiing, and golf.